Moments of
Grace

ALSO BY PATRICE GAINES

Laughing in the Dark

Moments of
Grace

✦

meeting the challenge to change

PATRICE GAINES

Three Rivers Press
New York

Permission to reprint the correspondence on page 159 is courtesy of Bernard Sauve.

Published by Three Rivers Press, a division of Crown Publishers, Inc., 201 East 50th Street, New York, New York 10022. Member of the Crown Publishing Group.

Originally published in hardcover by Crown Publishers, Inc., in 1997.

First paperback edition printed in 1998.

Random House, Inc. New York, Toronto, London, Sydney, Auckland

www.randomhouse.com

THREE RIVERS PRESS and colophon are trademarks of Crown Publishers, Inc.

Printed in the United States of America

Design by Linda Kocur

Library of Congress Cataloging-in-Publication Data

Gaines, Patrice.
    Moments of grace / by Patrice Gaines.—1st ed/
       p.   cm.
      1. Conversion.   2. Conduct of life.   3. Gaines, Patrice.
I. Title.
BV4916.G35   1997   96-25404
170'.44—dc20   CIP

ISBN 0-609-80171-6

10 9 8 7 6 5 4 3 2 1

IN MEMORY OF ELEANOR AND BILL GAINES,

WHO GAVE ME THE FOUNDATION

Contents

Acknowledgments

I must always thank those people who sustain me with their love: my husband and friend, J. C. Thomas; my daughter and friend, Andrea Johnson, and my son-in-law, Norman Johnson, who is a new blessing to my family; my step-daughter, Endia, who reminds me to bend low, talk softly, and open my arms wide.

Thanks to my sisters and brother for the love they give so freely—and for letting me write about their lives as I write about mine: Shelia Williams, Carol West, Debra Gaines-Spicer, Sondra Gaines, William Gaines Jr., and Vicki Gaines.

My sincere thanks to my new family who have accepted me with unconditional love: John and Theodosia Thomas, Veronica Cherry, Cindy Mason, and Michelle and Monica Thomas.

The wisdom on these pages is not mine alone, and so I must thank all of the people who shared their lives with me:

Carolyn and Stanley Scott and their daughters Sonja Scott Jones and Joceyln; Sister Ellen Marie Hager, Father Raymond H. Moore, Donna Britt, Vonetta Baker, Vicki Hauck, Bernard, Margaret and Fran Sauve; Gaile Dry Burton, Jewelene Black, Mike Vanderhurst, Richard Koonce, James F. Tiu, Ian Charles, and Bonnie Honora Hammons.

To all the men and women in the prisons I have visited, for all they have taught me and for allowing me to witness the grace with which they work toward change.

Thank you Yvonne Shinhoster Lamb—again—for editing this manuscript before I turned it over to the Real Editor; to the Real Editor, Carol Taylor, thank you for the gentle way you use your pen; to my dear friend and agent, Denise Stinson, who gives advice—on literary and nonliterary issues—always considering the Divine.

And finally, one of the best things about writing a second book is that you have an opportunity to thank the people you forgot to thank in your first book. I apologize and thank: Ron Grognet, who was my therapist and led me to truths that allow me to live and write with more honesty; my friend Jonnie Grant, who gathered together friends in Beaufort, S.C., who helped me remember.

Moments of
Grace

Introduction

Imagine we are weavers, each given a chance to weave magnificent designs, whatever our minds can fathom. Our threads vary in color, length, width, and texture. Some of us assume incorrectly that we have odd pieces, knotted, frayed, and therefore we believe we cannot weave or even conceive a beautiful design.

Regardless of how bad things may look to us, we must weave with great faith, enthusiasm, and joy! If we do this, we will see that even the frayed and faded thread can create a most glorious tapestry.

This is the way life is. We create our cloth with the choices we make, the patterns we weave, the thread we choose to add to those we are given. If at any time we do not like what we have made, we can change. We move one thread, and the entire cloth is changed. We move another. And another. Until we have woven a new fabric, or life, for ourselves.

The pain, the problems, and the challenges of life are like a frayed thread. We mistakenly believe that conditions such as abusive parents, being black in a country that honors whiteness, or scoring low on an IQ test can determine the beauty of our cloth. We can still weave beautifully!

Of course, if as human beings we could choose the life we wanted, we would always pick the path of least resistance, the road around pain. But by avoiding pain we miss out on profound lessons, the glorious gifts of grace.

*   *   *

To change is a mighty task, demanding faith, courage, and perseverance. As much as we may want to change our entire life at once, we cannot. We must make it new one thread at a time. We must be patient and focused, because even though we can alter our exterior—where we live, where we work, who our friends are—we must still do the hard work of transforming our interior.

We make one change after another after another until our tapestry is complete and we have woven ourselves a sweet and magnificent life. *Moments of Grace* is about that process.

In my first book, *Laughing in the Dark,* I recounted my own journey from heroin and abusive relationships to health and success. On my book tour, I was asked the same question over and over, in many different ways: "How did you turn your life around?" "How could you go from using heroin and choosing abusive men to become drug free, a responsible mother, and a reporter at the *Washington*

Post?" "Why did you make it when others didn't?" "What is your secret?" "What saved you?"

I couldn't answer these questions adequately because the answers are not so simple that they can be communicated in a minute or two. The truth is, *we do not all change in the same way.* We take different paths to arrive at different answers at different times. There is no one road map to perfection and there cannot ever be.

However, we must all meet some of the same challenges to change. We must deal with the same issues, though they may manifest themselves differently in each life. What is offered here is wisdom on what you must possess within to change, and a look at those areas of life we must all examine in order to make our lives better. If a road map to change existed, it would look like an old treasure map with a maze of paths and signposts leading to the prize. You could reach your destination in a variety of ways but not without first stopping at each signpost at least once—and sometimes, much to our regret, again and again—before reaching the prize.

Moments of Grace is about those stops along the way. Many of them represent Faith, Courage, Friends, Family, Work, and Self-Love. To reach the treasure, you must visit each, be challenged while you are there, ponder the meaning of the lessons you receive, and be tested again and again. The prize? Peace. Happiness. Joy.

The challenges of life are unending, but you can find ways to handle them better. Life can put many obstacles in your path, but the fabric of your being—woven by you—can stay whole.

You will cry for a while and you will hurt deeply—but not forever. Even in your greatest sorrow, you can find joy and healing.

* * *

I have existed in God's grace for forty-seven years. The sweetness of His grace allowed me to live, though I was hell-bent on destroying myself. I have survived shooting heroin. I have survived abusive men. I have survived being raped. I have survived jail. Looking back, I am sure that it was only grace that allowed me to learn from my mistakes and that eventually led me home.

The title, *Moments of Grace*, comes from my belief that by living through the moments when we face our ordeals, we receive grace: the wonderful lessons that are ours forever, that enrich our presence here and provide a layer of understanding we would not otherwise have. I say "receive," but grace is always with us. I think of it as dormant, waiting for our use and appreciation. But most of us do not think of it—until those moments. Our grace is enlivened simply by considering it. The more we recognize it, the more alive it becomes, until we are aware that we are living each moment in the sweet comfort of God's grace.

In the Bible and in other religious books, we find many stories about such moments of grace and the struggles and decisions that lead to them. But in our own world, in our own lives, there are many modern-day Bible stories. We have only to look to our neighbor—or even closer, in the mirror.

I wrote of such a moment in my life in *Laughing in the Dark*. The moment came as I received an award from the National Association of Black Journalists for an essay I had written about my life.

> Onstage, I felt as if God had reached down His hands and raised me up. It was a moment of grace. A voice in my head said, Now you see? This is why you shot dope. This is why you went to jail. This is why you were lost. So that you could one day go out and spread the word that there is no greater love than love of self.

In the midst of a challenge, we are called upon to muster all it takes—faith, courage, determination, and more—to change. While we are experiencing the crisis, there seems always to be a pause in time—and it is then that we must ponder a question, a choice, or a truth—and make a decision.

After we have made our decisions, whether they are right or wrong, there comes another moment when we are given an opportunity to learn from what we have just experienced. My realization onstage came after I had chosen some very painful experiences. But as I stood listening to the thundering applause of my peers I received a grace-filled moment that allowed me to grow spiritually even more.

*   *   *

A life without pain is impossible, so our focus should not be on avoiding it but rather on surviving and learning from it.

I have a girlfriend who is stubborn when it comes to change. She didn't realize it for years, but she resisted every opportunity to grow. If she got a new job, she refused to meet the challenges offered. She was always late and learned the minimum of what was required and performed only those duties that she was not afraid to try (because she might fail). She did only what she wanted, which means what she didn't fear. For the longest time she even refused to learn how to type—though she had the opportunity—because she said she didn't like it, disregarding the fact that it was a necessary skill in a growing number of jobs. She learned to type only years later, after she was older and saw her choices diminishing and found herself increasingly stuck in clerical jobs. By then, all opportunities to learn had almost disappeared, so she quickly tried to teach herself what she could, but she never gained any real proficiency.

She was extremely jealous in her relationships, never trusting and always wanting the person near her. Yet she never looked within herself to see her own needs or value. Her search for happiness—and the ways she chose to pursue it—was always outside of herself: a new job, a new man, a new excuse.

Don't get me wrong. She was not a bad person. She was kind and loving, fun to be around, and very trustworthy. But she refused to choose change. So what happened? She married a man who was equally as jealous. A nice, gifted man who also suffered from a crippling low self-esteem. Eventually, he had an extramarital affair and a child outside of the marriage.

His affair almost destroyed my friend. For the first time in her life she was forced to look at herself and to consider her own needs and the choices she had made in her life. Will she see all that she should? Will she even look in the mirror, or will she stand before it and still look the other way? Who can say.

I told her in the middle of her weeping, "This could be the best thing that has ever happened to you." I saw a moment of grace on the horizon, if she wanted it and could take the difficult steps necessary to change. In her case, she had always chosen the road around change and challenge. Yet life delivered her a blow she could not avoid. This is the way it happens.

I only recognized my friend's avoidance of change because I had walked a similar path. I had made the same mistake over and over, even in the face of one crisis after another. In my case I was very young, but still I did not work hard at life; I did not study it. I reacted rather than acted. I loved the first young man I found who would love me. Drugs were offered, I took them. It was inconceivable to me that *I* could control my destiny.

* * *

The wisdom we receive—even reluctantly—during these moments of grace does not always explain why we had to suffer or why something painful occurred to us. In fact, the wisdom may not even be comforting at first. But eventually it will change us for the better and ease our fears—if we accept its grace.

Too often we get caught up in logic, in always wanting to have a reason for everything. Perhaps there exist inexplicable things. Perhaps with God, there is no logic of the kind that we on earth desire. Perhaps there simply is. And yet, understanding that can often be enough.

My mother died shortly after my first book was published. Maybe during my darkest hours, I asked why. I don't recall. What I remember is grief, the tremendous pain and ache of missing a crucial part of myself.

One evening at dinner with some of my sisters, Shelia said she thought that the reason our mother died was so that we might learn from her life; so that we would not make the same mistakes she made; so that we could learn to be more independent, because we were so dependent upon her.

I thought Shelia was on to something, but the word *reason* didn't feel right to me. Later when I considered the conversation, I concluded that death does not need a reason. We will all die. Death simply is. I told Shelia, "I think Mamma died because she was sick, not in good health." For me, at that time I did not need a reason.

True, my mamma was just sixty-four, and I had hoped she would live longer. But if she had been a hundred, blind, senile, very sick, would I have still searched for a reason for her dying, or would I have accepted it? Death is a most difficult lesson. It will almost always seem unreasonable to those of us left behind by a loved one's passing.

But the gift—the grace—from my mother's death, and maybe from any death, is that we begin to ponder the life of the deceased in a way we do not and cannot while the person is alive. This may not sound like much, because we continue to desire the physical comfort and presence of people as we knew them. (This is a longing that comes with being human, and we should not be ashamed or have to apologize for it.) Yet I know that pondering my mother's life has been a wondrous, enriching experience for me.

When my mother was alive, my appreciation of her was hindered by my relationship to her—by our disagreements, our own selfishness, our busy schedules. We had a great relationship, but what stopped it from being perfect was life itself, the roles we had chosen and been born into. After her death, I invested hours in poring over every minute of her life I could recall. I would not have spent my time that way had she still been alive.

Did my moment of grace explain her death, or relieve my pain? No. But it changed my feelings about my mother. I know that when I think about my mother, what I remember is mostly the good. The easiest things for me to forget were the same things that kept us apart when she was alive.

As the months after her death rolled by and her birthday neared, the first birthday we would celebrate without her, I felt anxiety building in my heart. How would I be able to live through the day? How would I mourn? What should I do? When I woke up that morning the answer seemed so clear: as I made up my bed, I began to sing.

"Happy Birthday to you! Happy birthday to you! Happy birthday, dear Mamma! Happy birthday to you!" I sang louder and louder and I applauded for a long time, cheering my mother, giving thanks to God for allowing her to be my mother, showing my appreciation for the life she had lived and the joy she had left behind.

Later my sister Shelia and I went to the cemetery and talked to Mother. But somehow I knew that though I would come to the cemetery again (partially because I know my mother would expect that), on my mother's birthdays henceforth, I decided to dedicate the day from then on to doing some good in her name. Perhaps I will volunteer to feed the homeless, a service my mother did in the latter part of her life, or maybe I will talk to young women about how to change their lives. I just know that I want to show my joy on that day—not my sorrow. I want to say: "Your death has reminded me of the importance of love and your life was an example of that." I want to give thanks.

A crisis such as death forces change upon us, though we can choose how we will react. But most of the time, the impetus for change is not as final or as powerful as death and takes more initiative on our part.

We are all trying to improve our lives, even if we don't make the right decisions in our attempts. Sometimes we forget that everyone is struggling with change. We look at women on welfare, or teen mothers who have three children by three different men, or young men with guns, selling drugs on the corner, and we do not consider the possibility that they, too, may be trying to change.

When I visited a juvenile detention center for teenage girls shortly after the publication of *Laughing in the Dark*, I asked them if they had a favorite passage from the book that they would like me to read. I imagined they might find something familiar on the pages where I write about drugs, theft, abuse, or even being in jail. Without realizing it, even I had fallen for the stereotypical image of these young women.

One young lady woke me from my stupor when she quickly replied, "Page a hundred twenty-five." I had no idea what I was going to read on that page. But as I started it all quickly fell into place:

> We may not change instantly, because that's not how change occurs, anyway. We make up our minds to live differently, and then we do what we need to do to change all of the corners and crevices of our souls that need cleaning before we can reshape ourselves. Change is a monumental accomplishment, and it involves for each of us tasks that appear small, such as learning to put everything in its place in your house, or tasks that seem large, such as getting old friends out of your life and finding new ones. It is a long, difficult process that takes patience and perseverance, and along the way we stumble, but we never fall as low as we were before the moment we decided to change.

Of course! With the journey I have taken in this lifetime, I should have known that—contrary to popular belief—many people in jail, or in this case in a juvenile detention center, want desperately to change and are consumed by the idea. If only it were an easy thing to do. And who extends a hand to help them?

On another occasion, the same segment of the book was cited in a totally different arena, at a reception and book signing at Gannett, the publisher of *USA Today*. There, a young woman told me that everyone in her office had copied page 125 and had hung it over their desk.

Everyone wants a better life, but not everyone knows where to look for the answers.

Mistakenly, we think that once we change, the rest of our life is perfect and without challenge. But you only know if true change has occurred when you are tested. For instance, if you leave a man who verbally abuses you, you can definitely expect him to call you up spouting sweet talk and apologies. It's part of the process. Otherwise, how will you know you're serious about choosing a better life? You will know you can say no to him only when he is on his best behavior, so pleasing and kind you can hardly remember the other side of him, and you still say, "No, I don't want you in my life."

When I chose to stop shooting heroin, "friends" appeared at my front door offering me every other kind of free drug. Real change didn't come until I could say no to every drug and every "friend" who offered one. For a long time, the knocks on the door continued. Then one day, there was silence. And the sweet embrace of grace.

We are all given opportunities to change. Some of us seize each chance; most of us don't recognize all of them, and so some opportunities slip by. Don't fret. They will come again. We may have different issues and challenges to face, but most often they can be reduced to the same common denominator: we do not love enough. We have more fear than love. We do not love ourselves.

Still, to embark upon the path toward change, the first truth to face is to know that the road will be winding and bumpy, sometimes it will narrow and be almost invisible from the overgrowth of thorns and briar patches. You will be forced to get dirty, perhaps even to get on your hands and knees.

Even when you don't see the road, keep your eyes focused on where the road should be!

Why change? Because each time you take a step in the right direction, it sets up a domino effect until you knock down all the walls blinding your view of your goal.

No more searching for love, dodging a man's fist, arguing with your mother, fearing that your father does not love you, or worrying about things you cannot control. You will fulfill your greatest dreams, slay your worst demons. You will get the job you want, the occupation you desire, the nurturing partner who cherishes and respects you. I know, because I did.

In the end, the bottom line is: the person who does change is the person who wants to do it badly enough. Because only they will be strong enough to endure the challenges and growing pains that come with the process.

Face change dead-on. Be realistic. Change is not a place of comfort but a bridge built by faith and determination. What awaits those willing to cross is peace, happiness, and many more moments of grace.

1

Riding
the Wind

FAITH

◆

You will never make a change of any kind without faith.

In the midst of working on this book, I was struck again and again by my own fear. These "fear attacks" can strike at any time, regardless of who you are. This time my fear *mocked* me. "What makes you think you are qualified to write a book like this?" "Who are you to tell people how to live their lives?"

In the midst of dealing with this fear, I went to a Catholic church, Our Lady Queen of Peace, in Washington, D.C., to bid farewell to a friend who is a nun. Of course, it was no accident when the priest, Father Ray Moore, started preaching about faith.

"Faith sees the invisible. Faith believes the incredible; faith perceives the impossible," he said.

I knew he was speaking to me, but I am sure there were others who felt the same way. I left church knowing that faith would erase my fear. With faith, I would write this book.

There will be times when the light is so dim you can barely see the road in front of you. At those times, faith can lead you. Just turn in the right direction—*and believe!*

As a reporter, I interviewed two incarcerated men who had already served nearly eleven years for a crime they said they did not commit. I believed in their innocence on the day when they were sentenced, and I still believed them on that summer day in 1995 as I waited at a Pennsylvania prison.

I had come to talk to them because I was doing an article for the *Washington Post*. But that was really only my cover. I *was* writing an article, but I actually wanted to talk to them because I wondered how they were faring and if they had grown spiritually from their experience. It was an opportunity to learn from someone else's life, which is another one of those moments of grace that is a benefit of being a reporter.

I knew that substantial spiritual growth could occur in prison (after all, I had spent time in a jail myself and even longer in a mental prison of my own making). One of these men had been an armed robber and petty thief before going to prison. The other did not have a police record, but he was on the fast track, a real lady's man who, I imagine, was a hustler of some type. So I wondered if they had changed, and if so, how.

In the cavernous visiting room, I interviewed them one at a time and found two very different men. The first, a small, slight young man, had discovered God and through faith had concluded that prison was obviously where he was supposed to be. "I believe it was divined," he said. He had faith that profound learning would occur while he was there. Sure, he also believed that he would win a court appeal and be freed. But the faith that gave him peace was a faith in God. It allowed him to take college classes, study the Bible, the Koran, and other religious teachings. His faith allowed him a radiant smile in that stark, cold room.

The other man stood six foot seven inches and looked to be more than two hundred pounds of mostly muscle. He was a giant in the physical sense, but his spirit was frail, his faith small. He spoke in a hoarse, barely audible voice, a sound so thin it made me think he might vanish in a wisp before my eyes. He was frustrated and angry about the last eleven years of his life.

"This is no way to live," he muttered repeatedly. "And for what? For something I did not do."

When questioned about how he spent each day, he mentioned his job, the prison routine, and added, "In the afternoon, I go to my cell and cover my head so no one will see me. And I cry."

He had cried every day for the first seven years and nearly every day in the following years, he said. Before I left him, his eyes reddened, and as he spoke of the strain of his incarceration on his grandparents and his mother, he repeated, "Eleven years of my life gone for nothing" as tears fell over his cheeks and he bowed his head.

He was one of the most tormented people I have ever

met. I have seen people in pain from illness, in pain from grief, in all kinds of pain. Yet I had never seen a man hurting as deeply as this one.

What could I say?

Absolutely nothing. How useless my words would seem. Where would I start? How could I appear credible to him when I was going to hop into my sporty rental car and zip down the mountain roads, away from that bleak fortress that sat miles from any town, surrounded by nothing but flat earth and endless sky.

Later, I remembered that when I asked him if he read or studied, he said, "I cannot focus. My mind always returns to my situation."

What would have taken his mind off of his condition and allowed him to focus? Faith, I believe. It exists for that reason, to be the bridge to get us over to the next moment, the next day, to firmer ground, where we can learn and grow.

Clearly, the first young man had faith. He overflowed with peace, and therefore, I found him a pleasure to be around. If the prison doors had opened for him that day, I would have welcomed him into my home. Someone would have hired him. People would trust him.

The second man had misplaced his faith, as so many of us do. He was stuck on the thought that men and women had implicated and misjudged him. He did not seem dangerous, but it was difficult being near him. His pain made me ache.

I certainly could not criticize him for his disappointment or his misplaced faith. I do not know how I would fare under the same circumstances. Would I stand on faith? I hope so, but I do not know.

I thought of how often I had placed my faith in a friend, a lover, an institution, or a system. That kind of faith can only bring you pain and disappointment because human beings are not perfect. That kind of faith can help you build a prison of your own making.

But the faith of the first man was a supreme trust. It told him that even if on the surface life seemed bad, faith would continually show him a way not only to survive but also to live freely and fully.

He had faced his moment and responded with faith. He had received grace.

*　*　*

I spend a lot of time in prisons giving talks as well as working on stories as a reporter. The questions I am asked and the situations I see people facing have taught me many things.

I visited a Maryland juvenile detention center for teenage girls. That facility was the last pit stop before juvenile court gave up on them and sentenced them to stiffer penalties. During a discussion, one of the counselors remarked that some of the girls were baffled as to how they could believe that their lives would change if they followed a certain path. They wanted proof that making changes such as giving up drugs, finding new friends, and attending school would mean their lives would be better.

I was at a loss for words. Then it hit me: "Faith," I said. "Faith is the way."

I explained to them that faith allows you to believe in the unseen. "It is taking a risk on yourself," I said. I told them that just as they placed faith in friends and drugs, believing that these would bring them happiness, if they put their faith in the proper place they would get a greater return. I knew they were risk takers or they would not have been there, but they were betting on the wrong people. Their faith was too earthly, too limited. The greater the faith, the greater the return, I said.

* * *

I was visiting another prison, in Georgia, when I met a woman who said she had been drug free when she went back to the old neighborhood where she used to get high, to visit some of the drug addicts who were her old friends. What did she want? Not drugs. No, she thought she could help some of her addicted friends. But she also admitted she was showing off, flaunting her cleanliness in front of them.

In other words, she was not listening to God. She could not hear the truth that beats inside of us and is available to all of us who will listen. Finding faith is not about showing off or bragging. It *is* to be an example, though in a kind, healing way such as working as a counselor or teacher. But you know what happened: after a few trips back to the old neighborhood, she tried drugs again, which led to addiction again, and eventually to the prison where I met her.

She had walked into the lion's den while she was still a lamb. She was not strong enough yet because she had not developed her spiritual muscles. She did not truly believe.

She had not fed herself spiritually by finding what worked for her: a steady diet of reading? Going to church? Attending a support group? All of these things, or some of them?

We are quick to get our bodies in shape by jogging and lifting weights. We work out at the gym regularly to develop our muscles. But so often we forget that there are exercises that are necessary to help us develop our spirituality so that we can meet the challenges we face and surmount any hurdle.

The woman in prison took her journey back to the old neighborhood prematurely. She thought she had changed permanently because she wasn't doing drugs at the time. But she had not developed faith, had not done the hard work of changing. She had also not been tested. She was doomed to fail one day. It was just a matter of time. In her case, two years.

Even when we think we are fully developed and in great shape mentally, we need to continue our spiritual workouts. We need to attend those meetings that support the changes we are trying to make; we need to read books that remind us of real truths and of what is important. This world is full of distractions, and often they affect us, though we think they do not. The only antidote, the only way to balance this and cleanse our spirits, is by feeding ourselves with church, music, art, meditation, friends, and all of the positive influences we individually determine will help keep us on the right path. We must stay focused and keep in front of us an image of what we want our lives to be.

Faith can be the ounce of difference that determines whether or not you survive any struggle or challenge. But before you have faith in yourself and others, have faith in the Divine. When that faith in the unseen is strong enough, it will transfer to you unannounced. You will know only when you must meet the challenges before you. When you can walk through the lion's den unscathed, then you are changed.

*　　*　　*

Is faith any different from a positive attitude? My friend Donna Britt, a columnist at the *Washington Post*, says, "Faith is the ultimate positive attitude. But having faith is difficult in our culture, which is suspect of optimism." She also points out that thirty years ago the biggest box office sensation was Doris Day, "twinkly, sunshiney, innocent. Now everything is dark and dreary," she says. "We trust cynicism, which is antifaith. In the popular culture of today it is more difficult to attest to faith than to be lauded for your cynicism."

In her syndicated columns, Donna often writes about the "twinkly, sunshiney" parts of life, the ordinary blessings we generally overlook or are too busy to see. She sometimes feels as if she is swimming against the tide by pointing to reasons for hope in a world consumed with crime and populated by people who are afraid of one another. We are always searching for someone to blame. It is not cool to be optimistic or inclined to trusting in something you cannot see, or especially to talk about it or write about it.

"But you can't live on cool," Donna continues. "All the evidence points to faith as being the only sane way to live."

When we were babies, we must have known this. Anyone who has watched a baby try to walk knows that the baby doesn't care whether you think she's ready to walk or not. She doesn't care whether or not her legs are strong enough, her feet big enough, her balance sturdy. Something clicks, or perhaps the baby is just tired of watching everyone else walk. So stepping out on faith, the baby puts one foot in front of another, wobbles some, throws out her hands to balance—and walks!

Even if she falls, she gets back up. She will try again and again. Give her a finger to hold on to and she may try to run. She trusts with the least bit of assurance!

As we grow, we become more skeptical. We tend to have faith only in what we have seen. The more we see it happen, the more faith we have it will happen again. Some things we see happen so often that we take them for granted.

"It takes a certain amount of faith to get out of bed in the morning, to know that there will be a floor under your feet, air for you to breathe, that there are enough resources to sustain you in the most basic way," my friend Donna points out. "The more I exercise a faith that goes beyond these basic things, the more I see proof that faith works." She goes on, "I think if I gave myself over totally to faith, my life would be perfect. The farther I jump out on faith, the firmer the ground and the more beautiful the scenery."

My friend Vonetta Baker became blind at age fifteen.

At that very moment she made a deliberate decision to grab hold of faith. Now faith is so much a part of her nature that she isn't even aware she has it. That is the way it should be for us all.

She told me the story of a recent trip to Africa and how her group came to a stream that everyone had to jump over. A good friend was leading her and another was behind her. They tried to describe the width of the stream so Vonetta would know how far she had to jump.

Vonetta hardly listened before leaping. Only when in the air did she consider what she had done. "I yelled, 'Caaatttcch meeee!' " she recalled, laughing.

"You have so much faith and courage," I said.

"No," she laughed. "I just wanted to get over to the other side."

When it comes to being mobile, Vonetta keeps her faith with her at all times because she has had to use it so often. She does not doubt its abilities. She knows faith is the way she extends her hand to God for help. She reaches out to God, and He leads her, and she knows that when she stumbles, or falls, He will catch her, if she will let Him.

Yet that same faith does not extend so easily to other areas of her life, those not physical. Like most of us, she must focus more and make a deliberate effort to have faith.

*　　*　　*

For much of my life, I had faith in everyone but myself. I didn't think about God because I figured my faith in God was a given, that I didn't have to work on it or think on it. It simply was.

But we *must* focus on our faith in God to make it real. During Father Moore's sermon on faith that Sunday, he reminded us of the Bible story where Jesus asked Peter to step out of the boat and walk on the water toward Him. Peter did as he was told.

"Only when he began to wonder how this could happen did he begin to sink," Father Moore said. "He lost his focus on God, on his faith."

Later Father Moore explained to me that "The boat is kind of an area of safety. The sea represents life, and when the storms of life toss and turn the ark of our safety, we are threatened.

"As the boat is being tossed, Jesus walks on water, and we are asked to follow. But when we take our eyes off Jesus, we see the depths of despair and start to sink," said Father Moore. "How far we get depends on how much we focus on Jesus."

We all have our arks of safety. Some of us think once we have found our mates for life, we are safe at home base; we can rest eternally, forgetting about faith. Or we get a job that is the epitome of success in our profession, so we let out a spiritual shout—"I've made it, glory hallelujah!"— and we forget to continue to nurture our souls any longer.

I have a girlfriend who years ago used to write affirmations and repeat them faithfully. Her spirit was growing by great lengths, her confidence was improving. She was reading books to boost her self-esteem and planning to take classes that would give her an upper hand in the job market. Then she fell in love and eventually got married.

She changed, drastically, though so slowly that even she didn't realize it. She had stopped feeding her spirit. She no longer wrote or read affirmations. Her husband's goals became her only goals, so she no longer concentrated on what *she* wanted. By the time she woke up to what was happening, she had become such a bore that even her husband tired of her. Her self-esteem had plummeted and her career had quietly slipped away.

She found herself sinking. She had lost her focus—and her faith. For a while, she couldn't conjure up enough faith to believe in life—at all. She and her husband separated. But whether they get back together or not, she must become again that confident person with a zest for living.

I am sure one of the principles that helped me to turn my life around was my dedication to the process of changing. I kept my focus. I taped affirmations and other uplifting messages, including Bible verses, to my bathroom mirror, on the refrigerator, or on my bedroom wall. My daughter grew up reading them. But I was still in a state of confusion. I had affirmations on my walls and chaos in my heart.

We have all visited people like this. They have posters inviting us to love ourselves, volumes of self-help books, a huge Bible on the table, and yet they lie, cheat, steal, and act ungodly in many ways. I was such a person. I focused on God part of the time and then my attention was captured by something or someone else.

What I used to call faith in God was my belief that I could get something if I prayed for it. But if I had had real faith I would have known there was no need to be so *specific* in some of my prayers. I would have trusted God to know what I needed and to provide it, even without me asking.

For instance, after a year of dating a man, I wanted to marry him, so I prayed to God that we would marry. I said something like, "God, please make John love me and let us be married and live happily ever after."

I ignored the signs that John was not right for me. I put aside my "common sense," which told me I needed to change some things in my life *first*, before I joined with someone else. Later when I was married and miserable, I was reminded of what my grandmother used to say: "Be careful what you pray for; you just might get it."

John abused me, both verbally and physically. He told me I was nothing, not a good wife or mother. He disrespected me. He slapped me, put me out of the car once, and another time he tried to run me off the road while I was driving my own car.

Faith can stop your desperate search for a mate by allowing you to realize that when you are ready the perfect mate for you will appear. There's nothing magical about this. When you are confident within your self you breathe easier, you walk differently. Meanwhile, invest in yourself! Take classes, travel, buy a house, start your own business, grow spiritually. If you have faith, you will not be lonely. You may be lonesome at times, but you will always know that there is someone by your side.

When I was with John, I was suffering from misplaced faith. When you place your faith only in others you set yourself up for great disappointment. When you put your faith in yourself, you may feel disappointment, but faith tells you that what has happened is best for you, that there is a lesson to be learned. You come out victorious in spirit. Not beaten. Not bowed. Victorious.

In a real way, my misplaced faith nearly killed me. I chose men who abused me while I believed they held the answers to all my problems. They would make me feel better about myself, ease my pain while caring for me financially. But as human beings we must care about our bodies, they are our personal temples through which God works. We must care about our mental and physical health and our safety.

Too often women stay with men who abuse them. These women must be reminded—as I had to be—that it is God, not man, who deserves their uncompromising faith.

*   *   *

"God will give me the money to pay my bills."

That's what I used to say every time I overspent. I wrote checks on money I knew would not be at the bank for another two or three days. I made promises to debtors, knowing I could not meet the obligations I was setting.

The joke was definitely on me. The truth was God made it possible for me to get the money and trusted that I would use it wisely. The money was entrusted to my care. Of course, I always prayed for more money because I honestly and desperately needed more. But why should I be given more when I didn't take care of what I had?

We are each imbued with the ability to make the right

decisions when our moments come. We have free will—to spend foolishly or to budget wisely. If you want to change your spending habits, you can. If you want more money, you can always get it. But if you truly want to change your life, you must first take stock of your situation.

I was put in situation after situation that were examples of God patiently extending His grace so I could learn how to budget money. One moment I was an unemployed, single mother and had to beg social services for food. At another I was married to John, who took care of my financial needs, allowing me to use my own money for my benefit but making me suffer in many other ways. At another time, I was married to a musician who was not always employed, so I was the main breadwinner and budgeter.

A series of bad decisions, lack of faith, and living in total darkness led to my begging for food at social services. I chose drugs that clouded my judgment and sent me plummeting into an abyss from which it was hard to climb out.

I depended on other people, generally on men, for my well-being. Instead of studying, seeking better jobs, or saving money, I had faith that the men I dated would care for me and my child and satisfy me both physically and spiritually. I lived to find the right man. And when I didn't find him—or the love I so desperately craved—I used drugs to lessen my pain.

When I married John and saw he was abusive, instead of saving money for the hard times that were obviously on the way, I used my money to party, buy drugs, and smother myself in new clothes. These were feeble attempts to feel better, to help myself survive in the life I had chosen.

When I was married to Ziggy, the struggling musician, I couldn't depend on a steady income from him to augment my salary. Fine, I said. I was an independent woman. But almost immediately, I threw myself and my talents into rescuing his career. I could see what he was doing wrong and I would change it. He needed a manager; I became a manager. The band needed someone to do the bookings; I made the contacts. The band needed a place to rehearse; why not our house—and if some of the guys needed a place to live, well just move in with me, my husband, and my child.

Ironically, the talent that would have given me all of the money I needed, the ability to write about what is in my heart, was with me throughout all of this. But my lack of faith stopped me from seeing that talent. My misplaced faith made me focus on helping my husbands with their lives instead of developing my own talent. My lack of faith made my prayers small.

I envision that small prayers create only a tiny hole through which blessings can fall. Yet expecting blessings to pour through such a small opening is like waiting for a flood to pass through the eye of a needle. Trusting in the Divine and praying big prayers opens up the channel for blessings, turning a small hole into a large funnel through which good can pour into your life. In my small prayers I was asking for the lottery number (the man of my dreams) when I should have trusted God to show me that my riches lay within my own God-given talents.

A psychic once told me that people come to her to ask for a lucky number to play in the lottery. They demand a winning number because they believe wealth will end all of their problems.

She helps them with some problems but she refuses to give them a lottery number unless she believes God wants them to have it. Instead, she probably surprises some clients and angers others with her answer.

"God may want to give you your wealth in another way," she explains. "He may not want you to win the lottery. He may want you to meet your neighbors who will see that you are fed, or to make amends with your sister, who will invite you to come and live with her for free while you repair her house. He may give you a job at a clothing store, where you will be able to pick out at little or no cost the clothes for all of your family to wear."

Of course, many people walk away grumbling about her gibberish. They do not see the beauty of the life she has laid out for them. They don't ponder the thought that money can be spent, but good friends and love are forever and enrich the spirit in ways that money cannot. They do not stop to ask themselves if they are searching in the right direction for the answer to their problems.

Father Moore recounted for me the Bible story where God asked Abraham to go on the mountain and sacrifice his son, Isaac. Abraham and his wife had become parents at a very old age, and God had promised Abraham that his son would be the beginning of a nation of people.

"It seemed that his blessing was being taken away," Father Moore said. "Still, Abraham went to the mountain and prepared the fire for the sacrifice. Before he laid his son on the fire, Abraham looked up and saw a ram in a tree."

The ram was God's way of telling Abraham that he could sacrifice the animal instead of Isaac. "God still provides a ram in the bush when we believe our blessing is being taken away," said Father Moore.

My ram in the bush was writing, but I put my faith in men—in boyfriends and husbands—and I was gravely disappointed. It would have been wise to have had expectations, perhaps, or a limited amount of faith. But I put all of my faith in them and forgot to continue my own development or to put my faith in God.

Having faith in someone else is one of the scariest kinds of faith because we feel as though we have no control. We feel dependent upon someone else. If you ever feel that, know that your faith is misplaced. Your faith should be in a greater spirit than those on earth. Faith in God erases desperation and fear. It enables you to feel calm and safe.

The truth is people seldom act the way in which *we* believe they should. A child doesn't always listen, our parents don't always see things our way, and a friend may disagree with us on something we are so sure of.

Save yourself the pain. If your faith is in God then you will trust that any outcome is for your greater good. You may not understand it. It may still hurt. But in the end, if you are quiet and listen, you will hear the truth—and learn. You will be wrapped in peace. Your faith will sustain you.

*   *   *

God has faith in us, too. He has faith in our abilities, our thinking, our talent. If He didn't, everything would be done for us—as if we were children. God has faith we will discover our talents, faith we will learn from our mistakes, faith we will grow from our grace.

God has enough faith to allow us to make our own decisions, to weave our own design. If he did not have such faith, each of us would be given the same path, the same experiences, the same thread. In fact, we would all be exactly the same. Exactly.

Today, I have faith in the people I choose to surround myself, but it is tempered by knowing that they, like me, will make mistakes. They will not always live up to all of my expectations. They have their own agendas and lessons to learn. I know that ultimately my greatest faith must be in God.

*   *   *

Put your faith in God. And then listen. The more you listen, the better you hear. Be still. Hear the truth. The more you listen to God, the more you recognize the voice of the spirit inside of you. You come to understand that you can have faith in yourself and in your own judgment and your own decisions because you know that God speaks through you. When you are one with God there is no difference between trusting yourself and trusting God.

But the state of being one with God can be difficult to obtain—because we make it difficult—and so we vacillate: what is God saying to me? What does this mean? Is God telling me to take this job? Is God telling me to remain married to this woman?

We spend hours, days, even months second-guessing decisions or being paralyzed by indecision as we ask one person's advice, then another's. I have a friend who cannot make one decision on his own without calling a dozen people for advice. The last time he called me it was to ask whether or not he should quit his job. For years he felt mistreated, unappreciated, and disrespected. My answer was, "Do something! Take some action."

He has been in limbo for years. "What is the worst that can happen?" I asked.

"I could be unemployed and have a smear on my employment record," he said.

I reminded him that he is a single man with no pressing financial obligations. "So what do you want—a job or a career you love?" I asked. "Do you want a smear on your employment record, or a heart attack? Do you want to take a chance on living or just fade away from mistreatment?

"Have faith," I said to him, gently. "Have faith."

He hung up and probably called the next person. I didn't tell him what he wanted to hear. Clearly, he was afraid of making a move. Instead of faith, his heart was filled with fear. I admit I was a little impatient with him because I had talked to him so many times about fear and faith and his job.

He is still working for the same company, always complaining that he isn't paid what he is worth, constantly threatening to quit. Faith would allow him, like the baby, to take one step—and then another.

* * *

In the biblical story of Sodom and Gomorrah, God leads Lot and his wife, Sarah, from the city of sin before it is destroyed. But He warns them not to look back. They are to leave in faith, knowing that there is no reason to dwell in the past but many reasons to step into the future.

Sarah disobeys. Her one glance backward turns her into a pillar of salt. She is paralyzed forever.

Sometimes we dwell too long on the past because we do not have the faith to move along. One of my sisters was like this after my mother died. Her grief was understandable. We all grieved—openly and silently, passing through many stages, returning to some. But all of us looked forward, except this one sister.

She said to me, "I just cannot accept that Mother is dead." Her comment made me analyze my own feelings to see if there was some advice I might offer her about how I had been able to accept this death and move on. I realized that instead of looking back at the pain and sorrow of the moment when my mother left this earth, I had purposely made a decision to dwell on the ongoing joy that mother had left in our lives. I thought of the present and what I was left with: the effect mother's life had on me at that very moment. The grace of her passing.

My sister was paralyzed, unable to get dressed in the

morning, unable to look for a job. She was—in a way—a pillar of salt.

Faith, I told her, was the answer. "You need to understand that life is still good, that mother is well, that her spirit, her love, and her essence dwell with us. Even if you can't believe that yet," I said, "have faith and know it is true."

It is the same if we dwell on our past sins. You will never forgive yourself if all you think about is what you've done wrong, or you will never forgive others, if you constantly rehash what you think they have done wrong to you.

I thought I had learned to forget the past, but I was once again tested. For years I had lied on my job applications. At age twenty-one, I had been convicted of possession of heroin with intent to distribute. But in answering the question on job applications "Have you ever been convicted of a felony?" I wrote, "No."

Then after working at the *Washington Post* for about five years, I became involved in a lawsuit in which reporters were suing the company. Before going to court, I had to tell the *Post* management the truth so that it would not come out in testimony. Next, the company had to decide whether or not to fire me for lying.

As the days drummed on, fear overtook my faith. I rehashed my past and sank into an old definition of myself: I was a liar and cheat, useless, a no-good drug user. I forgot my faith in God and myself.

It was friends who pulled me back and reminded me of the truth: I was an honest, drug-free person, a loving parent, and a talented writer. Three months later, the *Post* decided to keep me on, and I was forever free of my past! That freedom meant I not only continued working at the *Post*, but it also meant that because I no longer had to hide the truth, I could write about my life. Eventually, that led to my writing my autobiography, *Laughing in the Dark*, and my being not only a reporter but also an author and a speaker. What would have happened if I had prayed only to keep my job?

If I wallowed in my past mistakes—in shooting heroin, in choosing men who beat me, in stealing and lying—I would forget the beauty of my own heart and the person I am now. When I wrote my autobiography, I was required to ponder for hours at a time some painful mistakes I had made and horrible incidents in my life. Each morning before I wrote, I prayed, "Let me write something that will help others. Let me see my past through love."

If I looked at those past transgressions through a prism of wisdom based on my present self, then I was not dwelling in the real past, I reasoned. I was not reliving those times. I was visiting them as a person different from the one I had been then. I had love for those who had abused me. I had forgiveness for myself. These were my saving graces.

* * *

Faith is free. It does not cost a cent. My friend Father Ray Moore likes to remind his congregation of Moses leading the people of Israel through the desert and the Red Sea. The armies of the pharaoh were bearing down, and all the people could see was the army behind them and the sea before them. Moses prayed and God said stand still.

"Sometimes when we are being approached by pharaoh's army, the thing to do is to stand still and let God work," says Father Moore.

It takes the greatest faith to do that. When Moses stood still he was able to hear God.

"Sometimes we are overwhelmed and our natural response is to react to things," says Father Moore. "What we are to do is to be still and listen to the Lord."

God asked Moses what he had in his hand, and Moses responded, "A stick." God instructed him to take the stick and stretch it over the water.

"Sometimes God asks us to do unbelievable things," says Father Moore. "God believes in us, just as we believe in Him. But sometimes we don't see miracles because we don't want to take the invitation to use what we have."

Moses used a stick to free his people. The sea parted when he extended his stick.

"We all have a stick, but a lot of people don't pick up their stick," says Father Moore. "With a stick, you can draw, compose music, conduct an orchestra, or hit a ball and break a record."

*　　*　　*

Faith is no good unless it's tested. How would you know you possess it unless you're forced to use it? We all want to proclaim ourselves saved, drug free, faith filled, loving—whatever wonderful adjective we choose to describe ourselves. But we don't know if we are drug free until a "friend" knocks on the door to offer us drugs and we say, "No thank you." It is the same with faith. We don't know it is real until a great challenge comes and our faith is tested. If your life is like mine, there will be many tests.

I have just leaped another hurdle, flown over another wall built by my own fear. But I remembered God's extended hand and I reached out my hand in faith. At first I grabbed hold of just a finger and I took a tiny step. Then I took another and another until I was running fast enough to leap, then to fly.

The end result this time was *Moments of Grace*. On faith, I wrote the words you are reading.

2

Square Shoulders and a Broad Back

◆

At some point, your faith will be tested and you will have to act. That action is called courage. The two—faith and courage—are like sisters, tied together by birth. Faith will give you courage when you need it.

One of the most courageous people I know is my friend Vonetta Baker, whom I mentioned earlier. Vonetta has never let her blindness stop her from doing anything. She graduated from college, served in the Peace Corps in South America, and is now a chaplain at Western Carolina Center in Morganton, North Carolina, a residential facility for people with severe and profound mental retardation.

Vonetta laughed heartily when I called her to say I admired her courage.

"I don't think of myself as courageous," she said, still laughing. "I don't have time to think about it. I'm too busy trying to remember to take my medicine, or turn off the stove. I simply do what I have to do."

She speaks in a thick, high-pitched lilt, her words laced in a southern accent, but not a drawl. She has the curiosity and playfulness of a child, and her pretty, round eyes are so large they seem to shine and almost make her blindness seem nearly unbelievable.

Vonetta knows you cannot talk about courage without mentioning faith. Though she is unaware of her own courage, she does believe she possesses great faith.

"The more I let go, the easier life is," said Vonetta. "Faith won't run away. When you learn that, you can jump over any river. It's a freeing thing."

When she was fifteen, doctors discovered she had a brain tumor. For a while, she lost both her hearing and her sight. The tumor was removed in emergency surgery. She does not know if her loss of vision came from the surgery or the tumor—and she's never cared to dwell on the question.

Youth was on her side, that energetic faith that comes from being so young you still believe in the impossible and not in a world that teaches you fear.

"Before surgery, I had a vision of myself in a wheelchair dressed in a brown skirt, with a black shawl over me," said Vonetta. "I was determined not to be that pitiful, disabled person in my vision."

Over the years, she has developed her own theory called "God's economy," which she uses to explain the availability of everything we need to have happy, successful lives.

"I believe God puts things like love, patience, kindness, faith, and courage where human beings can't capitalize on them," said Vonetta. "He puts them where everyone can enjoy them. If only some people could get them, they might sell them or use them as tools to gain power, or give them only to friends.

"But God doesn't make the beauty of the autumn leaves just where some people can see them, he puts them where even the disabled can see them. He puts faith and courage where we can all choose them—and if we do, just use a tiny bit at a time—faith the size of a mustard seed—it will grow."

Vonetta is used to people complimenting her by saying, "If I were blind, I don't know if I could . . ." Then they mention some specific act she has done—a speech, a trip abroad, camping.

"I say, 'Well it's good that I'm the blind one then,' " said Vonetta, breaking into one of her easy, booming laughs.

The truth is, she believes—as I do—that more times than not we rise to meet the challenge. We do what we have to do to survive.

"The real truth is they don't have to compare themselves," said Vonetta. "No one knows really how they would respond until it happens to them."

* * *

I once interviewed a woman who lived in the Virginia suburbs of Washington, D.C., who believed she was called by God to help women in a D.C. public housing development. I thought what she did took courage, and she tried to explain to me how faith propelled her into action.

The woman, Vicki Hauck, had read in a newspaper article that a three-year-old girl had been killed by a stray bullet from a gunfight in this drug-infested neighborhood. The article stayed on her mind, and she said she felt God calling her to go to that neighborhood to help.

I asked how she knew it was God telling her to go. What does a call from God sound like or feel like? What makes it different from a message from within yourself?

"When God tells you to do something, you don't think practical thoughts such as, 'Where is D.C.? How will I get there? I don't know these people.' You have none of those earthly thoughts that instill fear," Vicki explained. "You obey. You act on faith."

Because of God's calling, this woman had the courage to do what many people did not. She left her safe, middle-class home to go to an inner city housing project and recruited other women to go with her. After joining forces with a nun from a church in the Washington neighborhood, she formed a support group for the women who lived there. Through that group, the city women found the strength to return to school for high school equivalency diplomas. They finished drug rehab programs, found jobs, painted their apartments, set goals, and changed their lives.

Vicki's faith gave her courage, and her faith and courage multiplied and spread. Most of the women on one street were transformed, and the ripple effect was that other people's lives were changed, too. The women from Virginia were inspired by the city women, who maintained their faith, courage, and determination while facing many challenges the Virginia women would never know.

When I heard Vicki describe her faith in action I remembered witnessing a fiery car accident. I jumped out of the car I was in and ran closer to the burning car. I knew people were inside and I wanted to help, but I remember as I headed toward the car thinking: I want to do this, but if something happens to me, my daughter (who was a teenager at the time) will be alone. I stopped running, and like probably twenty-five or thirty other people, I watched in horror.

Only one man had the courage to move forward. He ran up to the car and pulled out a baby and another woman. One older woman died in the burning car. But he had saved two lives, and I was left to ponder every so often: Why couldn't I have pulled those people from the car?

Did he hear God talking to him? Did he simply act out of love? Did he run toward the car on reflex, without thinking? I interviewed him later, again using my profession to find out what my spirit longed to know.

I remember the man said something like, "I couldn't just stand and watch those people because I have children. I have a family. I would want someone to help them if they had been in that car. I thought about them and ran."

I thought about my daughter—and watched, convinced that if I wasn't a parent I would have run up to that car. But would I? I will never know.

* * *

Courage is not always physical. The first courageous step in your life may be a mental or spiritual one: the courage to change your mind—and your life. Courage can help you make a decision to stop living beyond your income, even if it means selling your large house to move to a smaller one; quit a job you hate and return to college when you're twenty or thirty years older than the average student; stop drinking alcohol and join a support group to begin your recovery.

In my journey, I have had to muster up courage many times. But perhaps my first step of courage was to decide to change. Sometimes making that decision means pitting yourself against all that you know, against friends and family or people who are your support system.

In my case it meant leaving old friends, including a boyfriend, my first love, and a young man I depended upon to give my life meaning.

Some people, standing on the outside, don't understand the courage it takes for a person to walk away from some destructive way of living. I was reminded of this when I saw a congressman on *Donahue* one morning. According to the congressman, the problem in America was the lack of moral values. People steal because they have no moral values. People kill, lie, rob, and use drugs because they have no moral values.

I don't deny that the problem has something to do with morals. But the other guests on the show, including writer Nathan McCall (who once robbed a restaurant and shot another young man in a separate incident), argued that poverty, unemployment, and lack of hope often play a role in whether or not a person chooses crime.

I agree. Courage, like faith, is only a theory unless it is tested. How could the congressman be so sure he would not rob someone if he lived in a community that looked like trash, saw working people still unable to feed their children, and had no skill or chance of getting a job? How could he possibly know that the moral values he has now would hold firm under such conditions?

Of course, many people do live righteous lives under such conditions. They are courageous people who choose to do the right thing even though they may not receive material rewards. But I cannot say I would react the same way. I do not know. I have been poor and I did not always choose to be courageous or to act on faith. I begged for food at social services and I slept with men I did not love so that they would supplement the small income I received so I could feed and clothe my child. I compromised my values in ways in which I'm still discovering. Unlike the congressman, I could not unequivocally say that I would not rob someone if I felt as hopeless as some people. I can only say I do not think I would.

We would be wise to teach our children not only moral values but also about faith and its resulting action: courage. In this way we would raise sons and daughters courageous enough to make the difficult decisions necessary to change our country, decisions that may not get officials elected but are morally right.

For instance, while I do not believe in the death penalty I do believe in jails. But unlike many politicians I do not believe that the answer to our crime problems is in building more of them or to hand out more severe punishment. I try to leave the punishment to God.

Jail, I believe, is where we, as a society, should have the courage to teach people to love; to show them that love begins with self, to work toward molding a person who loves humanity. That does not necessarily mean the prisoner should ever come to live in the free world again. But to teach a man to love is a blessing. To teach a man who has killed to love is a miracle.

We do not teach love by locking someone away to rot. That will not help us, the victim, or anyone. It takes much more courage to teach love. We have to dig far deeper in our souls to do that than we do to simply blame the criminal for his crimes and feel he has been punished.

It is here, in dealing with criminals—human beings— that I see one of our greatest failures as a society. Not giving love to people who most often never received love is a spiritual crime for which we will all pay. It is an act of cowardice, a lack of faith.

It takes courage to love people as they are. We won't all arrive at change at the same time. Not everyone is going to get a high-paying job, and we certainly are not going to make the right decision each time we are presented with a problem. In the case of the women's support group in Washington, D.C., there was one woman who did not stop using drugs even after the others had gone through rehab programs and committed themselves to change. When the Virginia women donated groceries to the D.C. women, this particular woman sold her groceries and bought drugs.

The group responded by telling her she could not receive groceries until she had committed herself to the beliefs and principles of the group. In other words, they said: We are here to help you, to lend our courage to you until you are strong enough to stand alone. They knew her kids had food to eat and did not need their groceries to survive, so they prayed for her and waited.

Eventually, she returned. And she abided by the rules, attending meetings, participating in neighborhood cleanups, going to drug rehab meetings. She took the first step of courage: the commitment to change her mind.

* * *

When I was growing up, I would fight for others, particularly for my family. Obviously, I valued them more than I did myself. But you must see worth in yourself to have courage to save yourself.

We all know someone who is in a helping profession— a teacher, counselor, or firefighter—who is always trying to save someone else but never raises a voice or a hand to protect herself. Though she may be seen as a courageous hero in the community, her courage falters when it comes to her own well-being. She does not realize she loves everyone else more than she loves herself.

* * *

We have a choice: either our courage (the product of our faith) multiplies or our fear increases. In my third marriage, my musician-husband and I decided to have a relationship that allowed us to sleep with other people outside of the marriage. We pledged to be totally open about this, believing our honesty would make the difference. The problem was that I was not being honest with myself. I started from a point of conflict because I did not really want that kind of marriage.

It was my fear that kept me silent, basically my fear of losing my husband. If this is what he wants, I reasoned, then I will oblige. I did not have the courage to speak up, the faith to know that I deserved to honor myself and my own needs. So did obliging my husband snuff out my fears? Of course not; my fears increased.

At times, I was jealous of the women with whom he slept. But my fear was not limited to the relationship; I was fearful of everything. Afraid other people would find out. Afraid I would burn in hell one day for my sins. Mostly, I feared that he would ask even more of me and I would have nothing to give.

And then my fear turned to disdain.

I hated him because he made my own flaws so obvious to me, the fact that I didn't have the courage to speak up. I believe my lack of courage destroyed the relationship, or at least did not give it an honest chance. What would have happened if I had not been silent, if I had said, "No, this is not the kind of relationship I want"?

Perhaps my husband would have honored my desire for commitment? Or maybe we would not have married? I missed an opportunity to be courageous and to have my courage multiply. I had to go through a maze of lessons before that courage would come to me one day.

* * *

When I was in elementary school I *knew* I was smart. If my teacher asked a question, I waved my hand in the air, begging for her to call on me because I was so sure I had the right answer. What changed to make me into a woman so afraid to speak up? I know that by the time I was in eleventh grade and in the first fully integrated class at a suburban Maryland high school, I seldom raised my hand. I was afraid to be wrong. My fear built a wall so high I could not muster up the courage to leap over it.

Somehow I interpreted being wrong as meaning I was stupid or bad. Wrong was no longer just a wrong answer. I was representing all black people—at least in my head. The weight was stacked against me and it pushed me over and crushed me under it. It was only years later, after I had taken several semesters of college courses, that I took the chance again of raising my hand.

Some things come to us naturally. It would not take courage if we did not have so much fear. Now I throw my hand up in the air, as almost a reflex, even if I just think I know the answer. It's fun to guess, to see if I'm right.

I imagine this is the way it is for people such as the poor who live under atrocious conditions yet maintain the moral values the congressman spoke of. Or people who we believe do the most miraculous things, such as my friend Vonetta. Because their fear is so small, they often do not have to leap. They simply walk across the waters—or even glide. So when you ask Rosa Parks if it took courage to refuse to stand up on the bus on December 1, 1955, and give up her seat, she may simply say, "No." She remained sitting because she was tired of living like a second-class citizen, and at that moment of decision, she felt no courage and, therefore, no fear. Yet, courage was there. It was simply a quiet courage, a soothing undercurrent that sustains our faith.

*   *   *

The world gives us all the reasons we need to choose fear over courage: your friends will reject you. Your parents won't love you. Your peers won't respect you. You might fail.

But we can't change the world as easily as we can change ourselves. Let the world think what it may. We can change ourselves simply by becoming mentally courageous. We just change *our own* minds because the truth is that our courage must come from *our own* faith. It doesn't matter what the world says because there is a faith beating inside us that will give us all of the strength we need to do what is right and to set us on the course of change.

It is courage that allows us to shoulder the responsibility for our mistakes. With square shoulders and a broad back, we do not blame our mothers, fathers, wives, husbands, or anyone else for our own mistakes. We understand there is really no such thing as blame. We are strong enough to face our challenges, whether they are an alcoholic or drug-addicted parent, growing up poor, or living with racism. With courage, we move beyond the cowardice of blame to a point of strength.

Courage is the muscle that breaks the restraining chains of blame—and frees us to move on.

3

Hands to Hold,
Arms to Lift

FRIENDS

◆

One of our greatest powers is "free will," the ability to choose who and what we want, or how we will respond to situations. With this glorious power we choose our friends, people with whom we will share our lives. If we understand the magnificence of free will—what a gift from God it is—we won't squander it. We will choose wisely.

When I was young I gave my friendship away easily, not valuing it because I did not value myself. No one had to earn the right to be my friend. No one had to prove their worth. I did not understand I was squandering a magnificent gift.

In fact, I thought that being picky meant you were snooty or arrogant or that you thought you were better than someone else. I did not believe it was compassionate or Godly to choose people. People simply fell into my life. I did not plan their entrances or celebrate them. I surely did not dismiss those who were destructive, or demand they make a U-turn right out of my life.

That was in the days when I had friends who taught me how to steal and shoot heroin. This was before I had watched my mother's friends gently bathe her tired, sick body so she might rest in dignity as she prepared for the departure of her soul. Before I had held the hands of friends dying from AIDS and realized they would become my greatest teachers. Before I really understood what friends do for each other.

Now I want people who will bathe me when I am too weak and sick to bathe myself, or who will wrap their arms around me when I smell of death. I want people who will neither harm me nor teach me to harm myself. People who will give to me what really matters most—love.

But that qualification demands that they know how to love, and when to love. And know that there are many ways in which love manifests itself.

* * *

Sometimes when you are working on changing your own life, you want to take your friends on the journey with you. When I decided never to shoot heroin again, I preached to my drug buddies the virtues of a drug-free life. I wanted, particularly, to save my daughter's father from the ravages of heroin. But friends seldom change at the same time.

Anyway, why should those friends have listened to me? What in my life would lead them to believe I had the answers? The only way I could help them was by example.

This was a truth that used to make me very sad. I wished I could walk up to old friends and take my hand and place it in the middle of their chest or forehead and pass on to them enough understanding, courage, and knowledge to make them new. The reality is, there are times when, as much as we want to help others, we can't help anyone but ourselves.

I had to separate myself from some of the people I loved, friends I had grown up with in my old neighborhood. Over the years, I would discover who had changed and who had not. I heard through the grapevine that young men who were like brothers to me were in and out of jail and drug-treatment programs. I saw them standing outside the neighborhood liquor store begging for coins so they could buy drugs and alcohol. I saw one standing in front of a shopping mall holding a paper cup and a sign that said HOMELESS.

Years passed and my hair turned gray at the temples. Then my mother called one evening to say that one of my old friends had died of a heroin overdose. I was shocked because I thought surely he had changed. He was a middle-class postal worker, married with children, a suburban home, and two cars. "How could he be shooting up and I not know?" I asked myself, knowing as I whispered that it was a ridiculous question. Our lives were separated by years of distance, and even if I had remained close to him, I could not have made him change.

I stood over his casket, asking, "What hurt you so bad that you could not stop?" I cried because my friend had not learned what I had learned.

It is painful to let go of friends we want to help. Yet there are times when we have no choice, when we need our energy and focus to work on our own problems. In the days when I had known my friend, I had been too weak to pull myself up; there was no way I could have carried him.

✳   ✳   ✳

Most of my longtime friends, who knew me when I was my old self (a drug user who hated herself), did not have the same self-esteem challenges, and so they were able to help me.

When I was badly beaten and raped by a guy I had dated, I felt so invisible and useless that it never occurred to me to go to the police. Why would they believe me? I was nothing and they would see that, I reasoned. I was a felon, having been convicted of possession of heroin; I was unemployed, a single, unwed mother—and on and on. But thank goodness my friend Anita Roseboro, never one to mince words, said, "You better get up off your ass and go to the police. You don't deserve to be treated like this."

She said it as gently as she has ever said anything. She was pleading, and in her face I saw the pain that should have been in my face. In the corners of her eyes, I saw the tears I should have shed.

"What he did to you was horrible," she said over and over until her words stirred up outrage in me. I was numb, frozen from the horror of what had happened, but I responded to my friend's hurt. When I could not feel, she felt for me.

In those old days, among my friends who shot drugs, I was the one who had gotten straight As and who used to be on the honor roll. I was the one who could excel in subjects the others dared not try. I read literature, tried different foods, had acquaintances who belonged to various ethnic groups. I was simply different.

Of course, this wasn't true in every case. But it was true often enough that later I would look back and realize I deliberately chose friends I thought were not as smart as I was. I was not comfortable around people who had gone to college, or traveled, or had experiences I had not. I did not have the confidence to be with them.

Actually, I had two groups of friends. I had those who were professional career people, and I hung with them until their presence evoked my sense of unworthiness, until my low self-esteem throbbed in my chest harder than my heart. Then I ran to my other friends, my lost souls who demanded little of me except that I share in their misery. My presence comforted them and theirs comforted me. But none of us challenged the other to grow.

I chose my mates the same way. I was afraid to be with a man who "intimidated" me with his intelligence. While I was a single woman in my twenties, I seldom ventured out of this mold, though I remember one particular case in which I did. I dated a young manager who had a college degree. I was nearly paralyzed with fear because I considered him such a catch. (In fact, I became frigid!)

I tell young women desperation has an odor to it. I am sure this young man smelled it on me and knew I was at his beck and call. But the scent of desperation must also become suffocating after a while. It was not long before this young man could not bear it. But I had not had nearly enough of him.

If he was late, I sat on his porch and waited. I even had the nerve to show up when he didn't expect me. He would come home to find me waiting like a lost pet. If the dishes in his kitchen sink were dirty, I washed them. If his apartment needed cleaning, I turned into his maid.

Would I have done this for an able-bodied girlfriend? Hell no! So why did I treat a boyfriend differently? Because I was desperate for the love of a man. I did not give the guy a chance to be a friend, and I was not a friend to him. Friends give friends room, the "space" I have heard so many men allude to in talking about relationships (though often it's their fear that is talking).

When this man corrected my mispronounced words, I crumbled. There, I thought, he really is smarter and better than me. I should have known not to step out of my league, I whispered to my dwindling self-esteem.

What would have happened if instead of lashing myself silently, I would have said, "Thanks for telling me. I've been mispronouncing that word for years." If I had treated him as a friend, I would have accepted his corrections as help from a friend. Instead, I turned his help into criticism, and a few weeks later, I was back with my old group of friends, looking around for a young man who I considered myself smarter than.

*   *   *

If we truly believe we are created in the image of God and capable of all things, then we know it's okay if someone knows something we don't know. In a healthy state of being, I know that if someone knows more about a subject than I do it's just because they studied that subject and I didn't. Nowadays, more often than not, I recognize that it is generally a subject I'm not interested in anyway. I know that I would be a bore and a liar if I said I knew everything.

While I may still not know how to pronounce certain words, I know how to write. When I didn't know how to write, I could type eighty words per minute—accurately. When I couldn't type, I knew how to cook a great chocolate pound cake. . . .

When we love ourselves, we accept that where we are at this moment is enough. Knowing all of this evens the playing field from which we choose friends. It puts us all on common ground, or on the same level, with everyone. It broadens the possibility of friendships, the pool of folks from which we will choose.

*   *   *

Once I had a male friend who loved me in a way in which no man had ever loved me. It was very unsettling. I was not used to being treated well, you could say. He bought me a car, a stereo system, gave me money for rent, listened to me cry over other men, encouraged my writing.

He didn't want to sleep with me or be my boyfriend. He was satisfied being my friend. But his affection confused me. Could I have a man who was a friend? A friend who gave me what I wished my boyfriend did? When my friend broke up with his girlfriend, and I was free, too, there was a brief period when we were both confused—or maybe we simply acted on what we felt. We slept together, and suddenly, we did not get along as well. The romantic, perhaps unreal, spell was broken. He was no longer perfect to me. I was no longer a mythical angel to him.

In this case, we both did the right thing and chose friendship over a bad physical relationship. We have remained friends for years. Sometimes friendship is the greatest of all possible relationships available to two people. He was the kind of "perfect" man who I once would have run from. I think his friendship saved me. Because we were friends first, I did not have to run from him. In a way our friendship circumvented my fears. Friendship is like that; it can heal, and it should make us feel secure and warm, like loose soft pants or an old worn bathrobe.

Though he did not know it, my friend introduced me to the notion that men can extend to women the same level of friendship that women can to each other (though they are expressed differently). I had never experienced such friendship from a man, so I misinterpreted it for passionate love.

*　*　*

There came a time in my life when I looked around and suddenly realized that most of my male friends were gay men. It was not planned, but it was perfect. I say that God in His grace put males in my life with whom I could not have sex. Whenever sex entered my relationships with men, I thought I was in love or at least the definition of the relationship became fuzzy. Was I in love? Where would the relationship go next? Was he playing me for a fool? These were the questions that popped into my mind once I slept with a guy.

The first of my gay friends was Cooper, a man so handsome it was a pleasure just to be seen with him. But it was our insatiable zest for life that tied us together. We loved to laugh, eat at fine restaurants, and party even on week nights. He taught me how to sneak out of work early and make it look like you were just going to the bathroom. (You leave your jacket on your chair overnight or leave it in the car at lunchtime and walk out with a pen in your hand, as if you're returning.) On the serious side, though, we were each very concerned about our spirit, about searching for a definition of God, and about serving our fellow man by doing volunteer work. We worked fervently to become good writers, and we both loved children.

Loving Cooper was easier than it had ever been for me to love a man. Yet there was a side of him he kept secret. With his silence, he taught me about the loneliness of being gay and being ostracized by society. I talked about my love affairs and he kept that side of himself private, though I knew some of the people he dated.

When Cooper got sick and was diagnosed with AIDS, our friendship intensified because love became more important. Preparing for his departure from this earth, I analyzed our friendship. I realized his love had made me feel safe. In some ways, he was a father to me. Though I was the oldest, he was my protector, always advising, scolding, nudging me to perfection.

Our last night out together, I took him to a wonderful Italian restaurant. Neither of us knew it would be his last meal. Looking back, I was glad it was a good one.

*   *   *

What attracts me to friends is a zest for life that manifests itself in spontaneity and a sense of humor. Also, I choose as friends people I come to admire and can learn from.

I met Michael, another gay friend, on a dance floor. He danced so wildly he came close to embarrassing me at times. Yet I admired his energy and boldness, his ability to feel free enough to move his body in any way that suited him.

We shared a love of literature and truly good writing. When he was dying of AIDS, I sat at his bedside and read aloud James Baldwin and Flannery O'Connor.

My friend John was as close to being a child as an adult can get and still be considered mature. He not only kept me laughing, but also kept me in awe of his capacity to treat each day as if it was the first he had ever lived. He had a love for life that was infectious, a childlike lack of fear that I longed to possess. He died at the Veterans Administration Hospital in Washington, but not before he attended his last advisory board meeting there, dressed in his pajamas and robe and rolling a rack carrying the bag from which he was fed intravenously.

Sometimes when I visited the hospital, he'd ask me to push the rack as we walked. Then suddenly, he'd take off running down the halls with me in hot pursuit, trying to roll the rack fast enough to keep up with his running. To John, this was fun. And it was! It was crazy, hilarious fun, and it spoke to his attitude about life: he was going to *live* until he *died*.

With the absence of sex and the confusion it usually caused me in relationships with straight men, I was able to develop deep friendships with these gay men. From them, I learned about men and maleness. I learned how good it could feel to have as a friend a man you could trust with your life, someone who made you feel like royalty, safe and secure, needed and wanted. In fact, I remember telling Cooper as he lay in the hospital, "I am going to use you as a measuring stick to measure all other men."

Some people would laugh and say, "How could you learn about maleness from gay men?" People who think this way are naive. Most gay men were raised as males and socialized by our society as males. But gay men had what I considered an advantage (though it was hard to think of it as a plus, since it came with abuse and prejudice). Like women, blacks, developmentally disabled people, and other minorities, my friends knew what it was like to be disregarded.

We were united by our oppression, by our self-hatred and desire to be like everyone else. At one time, we had hated our differences. Having these experiences made the gay men I chose as friends more sensitive, compassionate, and caring.

They became some of my greatest teachers as they died from AIDS—one by one—allowing me to sit by their beds and listen to their wisdom, learning from their lessons as they hurried to heal old wounds, to forgive and ask for forgiveness.

But it was my open heart that allowed the lessons to enter my life. This was because I did not judge people by their sex, race, age, or other artificial categories that separate us. Instead I measured friends by the amount of love they gave and by how hard they worked at being God-like. This made me open to the friendships of the men who would become my profound spiritual instructors.

My mother came to the memorial service I organized for Michael. I remember when I asked if anyone would like to come up and say something about him, my mother raised her hand. As she walked toward the front of the church, I imagined myself shrinking to the size of a five-year-old. The room seemed to shake with each step she took. I was transformed into the kid who is afraid her mother might embarrass her in front of her class. What on earth was she going to say? I sat down so I would not faint.

"I am not the most open person in the world. I am kind of old-fashioned . . . and I had to learn," she began. "But my daughter has always had all kinds of friends. Because of her, I have met some of the most wonderful people. Michael was one of the nicest. He was very respectful and good. He was always welcomed at my house. He came to all the family gatherings."

She was nervous. She stopped to take a deep breath. "I would like to thank my daughter for introducing me to her friends. I can tell you this—I don't know how well you all know her—but if you have Patrice for a friend, well, you have a real friend."

Then she walked back to her seat while I stood in shock. I felt proud not only of her but also of myself. The kindest thing she could have said about me on that day when I was full of grief was to call me "a real friend."

Later, some of my co-workers would tell me how touched they were by Mother's words. They knew that what she was really saying was that she had not always accepted gay people—but that she had learned to.

"Some of us sitting out there were feeling the same way—even though we loved Michael," one man told me. "Her comments kind of let us breathe more easily."

Yet my mother and father somehow raised children who welcomed as friends people from all races and orientations. I know that my acceptance has something to do with Charlotte and Lucy, the two young white friends I had in elementary school when my father was a marine, and also with living on a military base in a predominantly white neighborhood. I could never forget my childhood playmates, how they loved me, how we slept together at one another's houses and pricked our fingers to become blood sisters. This was before we learned the fear and prejudices of adults.

But what about my sisters and brother, who did not have the same experiences because they were so much younger than I when Dad was in the service? I believe the answer lies somewhere near the fact that my parents introduced us to all sorts of adventures, taking us to restaurants where we would be one of only a few black families present, to movies, Christmas parties, parades, everyday activities to some families but not to all. For us, these experiences meant we were comfortable anywhere and not afraid of anyone. (At least not afraid of people as a group. We all had our own personal fears to deal with.)

I think of this often when I run into black people who are afraid of white people and white people who are afraid of black people. Kids who grow up without experiences outside of their communities are more likely to become adults who believe stereotypes about people they have never met individually on equal terms.

I learned: you can never know from where your blessing might come. It might come from a white person or a black person, from a child or an elderly person.

I could not find a job after being found guilty of possession of heroin with intent to distribute—and spending much of a summer in jail. Whenever my police record was discovered, I was not hired, and at least once, I was fired. But when I went to apply for an office job at a mental health center in North Carolina, an older white woman decided to give me a chance.

If I had bought into the stereotype that all southern white people were racist, I would not have chatted so easily with this woman. Instead, we talked and laughed and she became the first person to hire me, knowing my record. She gave me a chance to start again. She would also become my friend and confidante. My daughter and I spent many evenings in her kitchen, where she plied my daughter with fresh biscuits and me with mature, womanly wisdom.

I have always had girlfriends who are white. I mean good friends who are like sisters to me. They have enriched my life, and our friendships remind each of us how silly it is to let prejudice separate you from the possibility of great friendship and learning. What allows us this possibility, I believe, is that we accept the truth that there are cultural differences between us, that racial differences may indeed enter into the friendships sometimes. But we don't find this frightening. We consider those times a chance to teach each other and to learn from each other.

Once someone becomes a good friend of mine I always have a difficult time remembering how we met. My friend Fran Sauve, one of my best friends, is a white woman who has been adopted by all of my siblings as a sister, too.

I don't remember when our friendship was sealed, but I know she is one of the kindest, most compassionate people I have ever met. There is a gentleness to her soul that soothes me. I remember watching her sit on my parents' back porch during cookouts, when she would deliberately sit and talk to my father. My father was not a communicative man, even to his children. Days could go by without him speaking. He never said "I love you" or showed emotions. Yet his face lit up whenever Fran entered the house. I noticed this gentle gesture on her part, and it touched me.

Several months after I was hired at the *Washington Post*, my grandmother died. I was sitting in the church at the wake when I looked up to see Fran, who is Catholic, praying over my grandmother's body and giving the sign of the cross. I was surprised and delighted. Few people at my workplace were aware that my grandmother had died. I didn't even remember telling Fran and didn't expect anyone from my job to be present. But there she was—the only white person at my grandmother's funeral. I smiled because, as I would tell Fran later, my grandmother was never particularly fond of white people.

The more I learned about Fran, the more I admired her. She was a volunteer at a local hospice, and I have long admired anyone who could do such work. When she was promoted, I watched the way she treated those she supervised. I admired the care she gave each person, the concern she sincerely felt for their development as writers and reporters.

She was a friend to the people she supervised, and my friend Cooper was one of those people. Cooper was convinced she was an angel on earth, and when he was dying of AIDS and I watched her wipe his brow and feed him, I was convinced, too.

Fran and I talk about God almost daily, and she has that zest for life that makes her live each day as if it is a tender gift. We have driven through winding country roads blasting Patsy Cline on the radio. I have watched her cut the hair of a black teenage boy visiting from Brooklyn. She even gave him the popular "scratches" or designs in his hair. The experiences we share are not unique to being either black or white but are defined more by our shared openness to life. Perhaps the greatest lesson I have learned from her is that we are all more alike than different.

* * *

In my twenties, when I was living an unhealthy life in many ways, I thought I had the most loyal friends. My mother and others concerned about me often said, "You need to change your friends." The problem was I was afraid to live without my friends. Where would I find new ones?

When we advise people to change friends, we don't understand what a difficult feat that is for some, how dependent they are upon those friends, how intertwined their lives are.

The first time I tried changing friends, I felt as if I were walking on water and about to sink and drown. Where was my safety net? My friends looked after me, I thought. Who will step up to fill their empty places?

In actuality, someone was probably telling my friends to get rid of me, too. We all needed help. I gave them drugs; they gave me drugs. We stole together. They were desperate to find men to feel whole; I cheered them on. If I were honest, I would have admitted that the basis for our friendships was: misery loves company. We cared about each other, but also we were glad for each other's company in our miserable state. We comforted each other with our presence. We were a pity party. We complained about white people, about men, about being poor, and about how everybody did us wrong. We echoed each other's unhealthiness, and in our chorus, we did not feel so lonely or alone.

I could not say no to my friends, which was one sign of unhealthiness. When I was broke, I gave them money. When I had little food, I held parties at my house and let them eat what food there was. I was buying friendship, keeping it the only way I knew. I bought them gifts when I could not afford necessities.

I wanted everyone to like me. If they did not, I felt rejected and I would slip into a depression. I am sure that if the notorious youth gangs of today had existed then, I would have joined them to spare myself the pain of rejection.

Yet when I decided to change, the first reaction of these folks I called friends was "She thinks she's cute now." At first, I let that little insult hurt me. Where were the great friends I thought would never forsake me? Could they suddenly dislike me because I was trying to get my life together?

I hurdled the pain of feeling rejected. I held on tight to the idea of change, looking down at my little daughter for inspiration whenever looking in the mirror did not spur me on. I was spending more time in places of change: at a community college, at church, in a job-training program. There had been a time when I had felt I would never find friends, people who had traveled journeys similar to mine, in places like that. But I discovered that when I took the time to look beyond the appearance of folks, I found some who were "cool," people who had overcome all kinds of challenges.

The longer I stayed committed to the idea of change, the more my life moved in the right direction, doors opened, and new friends stepped forth.

* * *

I met my friend Gaile Dry Burton through someone else and we became roommates. It was a period of my life I call "the bridge," when I was moving from one lifestyle to another—or trying. Gaile helped build that bridge. We rented a house together, raised our girls, shared a love of books and art and began to study and concern ourselves with our spirituality. We meditated and prayed together. We passed on to each other books on philosophy and religion.

Gaile was different from my old friends. Sometimes she teetered on the brink of right and wrong, too, but she always wanted to do the right thing. She wanted to change. We helped each other be better. We remain friends today, still growing and sharing our lessons.

Shortly after high school, I met my friend Jewelene Black, who everyone calls "Gobbie." I would be in and out of her life as I moved around the country, but always she remained my friend, so close to me and my family that she, too, is like a sister. When I was wild, Gobbie gave my life leveling. She is what some old people would call "an old soul," someone who always seemed older than her years.

Outwardly, our lives look different, but over the years

we've come to know that we are very much alike in our souls. She has been married to the same man since the age of seventeen, some thirty years. I, meanwhile, am in my fourth marriage. Still, we have experienced many of the same growing pains within our relationships. We have discovered when we loved our mates more than we loved ourselves and we have learned to honor the God within so that we could love ourselves more. Watching her is like seeing myself in a mirror—with everything in reverse. And yet, we are the same.

She has a quiet way, a grace about her. I've lived a good deal of my life screaming and kicking—showing my pain in my behavior. She has hidden her pain. As we've aged, I've become quieter and she has become more verbal, but we are still true to our old selves.

I remember a few days before a scheduled vacation in Germany, Gobbie discovered she had a lump on her breast. The day she was to leave, she had an appointment with a doctor so she could learn whether or not the tumor was cancerous.

"I'm taking my suitcase with me," she said. "If it's not cancerous, I'm headed for the airport. If it is, I'll be back home by three o'clock."

At 3 P.M., I dialed her number, hoping she would not answer, hoping she was boarding that plane for Germany. The phone rang. Then rang again. On the third ring, she answered. For a few moments, there was silence because we both knew what this meant.

"I never wanted to *not* hear your voice as badly as now," I said as tears dripped down my cheeks.

My friend had cancer. I watched her valiantly fight with an egotistical doctor who did not want her to get a second opinion. I watched as she took charge of her health and treatment. The silent one was roaring.

Since that time, six years ago, she has had one other bout with breast cancer. But she is still roaring.

* * *

What do all of my friends have in common? A zest for life, a certain attitude that says, "I will live each day to its fullest and not worry about which will be my last." My gay friends did this even as they were dying.

They all have a sense of humor, which I believe is a by-product of that love for life. They laugh a lot and their laughter is infectious. They are a joy to be around.

They all searched or continue to search for spiritual meaning in their lives. Some are churchgoers, some are not. But they honor God and treat their neighbors as they want to be treated. They are kind and compassionate and welcome into their lives people of different races, occupations, and social status. I say they have "large lives," brought on by a profound curiosity about life and people, and arms that embrace all that is good.

Every one of them has made me feel needed and wanted. They cherish my friendship, and it is important for each of us to feel we are needed. We want to know we make a difference in a person's life.

When my friend Cooper was dying I had not yet experienced witnessing a death, so I asked a priest what I should say to him. The priest said, "It is important to tell him what he means to you. Tell him what a difference his living has made to you."

*　　*　　*

When I was a child and my father, a marine, got orders, my family would have to move quickly to another city. I always envied people who had friends they had gone to school with from kindergarten through high school. I thought this meant their friendships were stronger because time had not separated them. Then as an adult, I learned that you could be separated from friends and still have intense, meaningful relationships.

My friend Mike Vanderhurst tells me he still tries to live up to the trust and faith his friend LeRoy had in him. LeRoy, who was in the navy ROTC with Mike, died in March of 1980.

Mike is a man who still carries his military training with him in his board-straight walk and in his tightly reserved emotions.

But this is how he told me of LeRoy: "I was a freshman in college, and although I was eighteen, I looked and probably acted much younger. We were all in the navy ROTC, which pretty much made us the nerds on campus.

"My best friend was a pudgy—no, a fat—kid from Philadelphia, named LeRoy. 'LeRoi' means 'the king' in French, something LeRoy would never tire of mentioning.

LeRoy could not run very fast, and he always finished behind the females—when he did finish—in our daily fitness exams as freshman. He was obstinate and hardheaded, in short a perfect candidate for the marines. And true to form in three short years, LeRoy would become a lean mean fighting marine, and would soon be outdistancing our best runners.

"I still think about LeRoy every single day. In flight school his T2 aircraft crashed. I never got a chance to say good-bye, as my ship was floating in the Persian Gulf."

Mike sent LeRoy's Mom a telegram on March 10, 1980. It read in part: "LeRoy was the best friend I ever had. His dreams were mine, his spirit will always walk with me. I know he'll be looking out for us somewhere, and I can only hope that I live up to his memory."

Mike refers to March 10 as "the day the king's plane fell to the earth." To this day, he tries to live up to LeRoy's admiration of him. His friend's belief in him spurs Mike to work hard to serve his family, community, and humanity. In other words, LeRoy is still very much alive in Mike's life.

* * *

If it is true that we carry our friends in our hearts, you must consider: who do you want in that most sacred part of your soul? Who are the people in your life? What do they teach you? Do you admire and respect them?

Our friends are like our mirrors. In us they see themselves, and in them, we see ourselves. We are different and yet we must be alike. To choose friends based on race or age or sex is to cut yourself off from the possibility of great lessons, to decrease the channels through which you might learn. We need all the teachers we can get!

The person you date and the person you marry or sleep with must be your friend. My mother was my friend and my daughter is a great friend to me now. Both have lifted me with their strong arms and held me when I was too weak to walk alone.

There is a poem called "Footprints" that is about someone questioning whether God was present or not during a difficult time. God responds by pointing out that at those horrible, painful, stressful moments, when the person walked the beach to ponder life, there was only one set of footprints in the sand because God was carrying this troubled person on His back.

I believe that at those times, too, God may implore the help of a friend, someone with strong arms to lift and hands to hold. Friends willing to say, "Jump on my back. I'll carry you until you are strong enough to walk again."

4

Lessons of Kin

◆

We are born into human laboratories called families. What happened to us in our beginnings, under the roof we called home will affect us all of our lives. No matter how far we travel, how fast we run, we carry home with us wherever we go.

Many times we leave home carrying heavy suitcases packed with misconceptions and anger, with feelings we should have expressed.

I fled to North Carolina shortly after high school, running from a strained, confusing relationship with my father and from my mother's rules. I ran because I wanted independence, but I took all of my pain with me. In search of my father's love, I gave myself to any man who said, "I love you." I carried with me my evolving image of myself as my mother's keeper and confidante. So when my sisters called to say my father had hit my mother, I hopped back into my little Toyota and drove the highway for nearly eight hours to arrive at my parents' house to rescue Mamma.

I had left home, but indeed I had taken home with me.

We can, however, decide how the experience at home will affect us. I could have continued to make the same mistakes over and over again, walking around with old grudges and misunderstandings, suffering from an aging definition of myself. But I wanted to change, to live a better, less cumbersome life, so eventually I chose to see a therapist. For two and a half years, my therapist led me through my past and my present. It was like cleaning out a closet overflowing with useless, outdated items and keeping only the really necessary things.

Before therapy, I had moved back home, back to Washington, D.C., and I jumped right back into my definition of me as "the fixer," calling together family sessions where I hoped to straighten out all of the internal spats I noticed brewing between some siblings. By the time the first—and only—session ended, two sisters were crying, several were cursing, and a fight almost broke out. Of course, I thought it was everyone else's fault, specifically because they could not see the truth, that they should all just get along.

I was blind to what they were showing me about myself. In other words, I was blind to what my being a member of this particular family revealed to me: I could not *make* any of my sisters change any more than they could have spared me from heroin or jail. We could love each other at the points where we stood, and encourage each other to change. That was all.

I know I am not the only person who has raised her arms in a gesture of giving up and asked, "Okay, God, why did you make me a part of this family?" At some time or another, we have all been irritated and downright angry with the very people who share our blood. I used to think my family was the craziest, sickest, most inconsiderate family on the planet until I paid closer attention to my friends, who complained of families that sounded frighteningly similar to mine.

No matter what example of family insanity I offered, it seemed someone I knew could match or top it with a story from their family. And I'm not talking about just funny, loony things, but serious, unhealthy behavior, too. Granted, there are many people who come from families with problems I have never known such as sexual abuse and other severe forms of mistreatment. But we often only think of the extremes—the abusive or the perfect (which only exist on TV or in our heads)—and think our families must fit into one mold or the other. Actually, the norm is in that large gap in the middle, which leaves room for them to sway toward one extreme or the other at any given time.

*   *   *

I am the oldest of seven children, and for too many years I let that be my burden, though I didn't realize it. I didn't know how to let anyone in the family do anything for me. I was the one who did everything because I was the oldest. That was a fact. The way it should be, I told myself.

I organized the family cookouts, coordinating who would bring what dish. I was in charge of collecting money to get gifts for our parents.

But it is in the family that we learn our roles and worth,

and so, I transferred my definition of being the oldest to relationships outside the family, too. I could not accept help from others. I wouldn't allow people to do something for me simply because they wanted to. I did not know how to accept.

Only recently, at the age of forty-six, did I have the faith to let go and let others in the family do their part in organizing a wedding reception for my brother. I instructed everyone to meet at the banquet hall on a Saturday at 10 A.M. to decorate. At 11 A.M. my girlfriend Gobbie and I were still waiting for my five sisters to show up.

If something like this had occurred in the past (and it did often because my family is not the most prompt), I would have been enraged. I would have waited until they showed up just so I could fuss. I would have been in a funk, worried that the event wouldn't go off on time—or well.

But this time, having learned something over the years about what I can and cannot do, I just left, leaving behind a note: "Please put tablecloths on the tables, tack a balloon to the center of each one, and put a candle on every table."

I didn't wait for my sisters to show up with the table-cloths, the wedding cake, the other decorations, or their helping hands. I closed the door on an undecorated banquet hall, trusting that when I returned less than five hours later it would be beautiful—or still undecorated, but knowing that I had done all I could do, and therefore, there was nothing to worry about.

Of course, when I stepped back into that room an hour before the reception, it had been transformed and was very festive and lovely. The balloons were in place, the wedding cake was on the right table, the candles were lit. And I, after resting and not having a worry in the world, was ready to party.

I was freed from that smothering, burdensome definition I had too long given to my position as the oldest. Also, I was free from believing that only I could handle something, organize an event, or do it right. That attitude also comes with being the oldest—if you let it. In fact, they did not follow my instructions fully for the reception but instead improvised using their own talents, and I discovered their suggestions worked better than mine.

I am sure that the freedom I felt, that the lesson learned, will now get transferred into certain situations outside the family. Yet the truth is I have never felt as adequate in the outside world. In the family I felt at least empowered by the position I was born into, and I sometimes wonder if that is anything like what it feels like to be born white. As an oldest child, I believed I was born to fulfill a certain role. In this case, to become a sterling example for the other younger children, to serve as a link between them and my parents, interpreting the wishes of my parents and organizing to make sure these wishes were met.

It is an imperfect analogy, I am sure, but sometimes I think in the Family of Humankind, Caucasians believe they are the parents, the caretakers and organizers. They know what is best for the rest of the family, what the others need to be happy. What I have discovered in my own family is that when you release yourself from that limited definition, you also free up everyone else to use their own talents. I can now better appreciate the smarts, wit, and creativity of my other siblings and trust that they are as capable (or more capable!) as I am.

*　*　*

Whenever we begin to change our lives, we have to look at what has happened or is happening to us inside our first family. Even when we think we are not affected by something that happened to us at home, we are.

Much of my life was shaped by my perception of my father's love—or lack of it. I thought he did not love me, and it hurt me terribly. I recall as a teenager having a screaming argument with my mother in which I proclaimed something like, "He is not my father! A father loves his children! He doesn't love me! He just takes care of me!"

I must have been about fourteen. I didn't know that it was important to say what I was feeling: "Daddy never hugs me or has never said, 'I love you.' And I want that." What I did understand was I was in pain, and I usually screamed silently, through my rebellious and self-destructive behavior. I hooked school, ran away from home, and loved wild, abusive young men.

The truth was: my father loved me, but he didn't know how to show it in the way in which I wanted. And I didn't understand any interpretation of love that wasn't illustrated on TV. On television shows, the children ran to the father when he came through the door. They bounced on his knees and he played ball with them. In my house, when we saw Dad come through the door we looked up and spoke to him. He never played ball with us, and we bounced on his knee until we were old enough to walk, then we were on our own.

But he loved us—and my inability to see that meant I operated under a misconception for years until I was willing to look again. That look came through my choosing to enter therapy.

My therapy freed me to see the truth—and my life changed. I was able to heal that relationship with my father, which freed him, too. He died shortly afterward.

My relationship with my mother was drastically and wonderfully different from my relationship with my father. My mother's love was a given. She never held back emotionally. She hugged, kissed, and said, "I love you." She was there when I needed her and always let me know that she supported me in whatever way I needed.

But I went through years of defying my mother's dreams and wishes. When I crawled out of my destructive life, I did so filled with choking guilt because I had not been a good older sibling, an example for my sisters and brother—and I had not been a good daughter. I carried that guilt for years, forgiving everyone else but forgetting to forgive the most important person: myself.

When I looked at my mother it was with eyes burdened with that guilt and through the veil of wanting to pay back my mother for all she had done for me. So there came a time when my mother could do no wrong as far as I was concerned. I owed her my devotion and protection. In every argument with my siblings or my father, she was the victim—always, in my eyes, and I took her side.

Looking back, I still believe that my mother was often a victim. But now I see that she chose to be a victim, that there was much about her life she could have changed, if she believed she could, or sometimes if she just took the initiative to do the hard work of changing.

Growing up, though, I did not see this. What it meant in the family was that it was always me and Mamma against everyone else. My sisters and brother stopped telling me about problems they were having with Mamma because they knew I could not hear them or their side. My father, who already had a tenuous relationship with me, wrote me off as hopelessly blinded to my mother's faults. This just added more tension to the problems he and I were already having.

I became my mother's caretaker. Again, as the oldest I felt it was my duty. My siblings were too young to understand or see life the way I did, I reasoned.

Slowly, my error was revealed. Once, I believed I had found the solution to all of my mother's problems. By this time, my father was an alcoholic, drinking every evening then sitting in front of the television until he dozed off and got up to go to bed. My mother, I figured, was a "co-dependent." At the time, this was one of the latest terms being used by people in the health professions to define people in the alcoholic's life who unwittingly assisted him in his indulgence. I found a group for "co-dependents" and gave my mother the information, assuming that once she read it she would attend the group therapy program—and *voilà!* her life would be changed.

I assumed wrong. My mother looked at me and said, "I've known about those groups for years. They tried to get me to go to them a long time ago. But I told them, 'There's nothing wrong with me.' It's your father who has problems."

Bam! Right up side my head. Another lesson. I could not fix my mother's life, take care of it or her, protect her from anyone or anything. I could not learn her lessons for her. And most of all, I could not protect her from herself.

I stepped to the side. But not far enough. There would be other bams up side my head before the lesson took hold. I did not owe my mother for my mistakes, any more than she owed me for hers. We both had to tend to our own lives, and I had to let my siblings work out their problems with Mother also.

Once I stepped to the side my relationship with my sisters and brother changed, too.

"You're no longer Mamma's gofer," my sister Carol commented one evening.

Everything was more in balance because my old misconceptions were not weighing the scale. My siblings could take my opinion and advice more seriously, trusting that it was not colored by my blind devotion to my mother. My new attitude made my siblings consider therapy.

"I've noticed the difference in you since you started," Carol said.

Sometime later, in my therapy sessions, my one-sided,

prejudiced look at my mother was replaced by a more balanced one, painted by the truth. My mother, like me, had done many things wrong, had not always acted on the highest principles or been courageous enough to take the hard steps to change.

For a brief while this truth made me angry with her, so that when she confided in me I would snap at her and be facetious in my answer. But as I learned, I actually became more compassionate toward her. Compassion was more realistic than the she-could-do-no-wrong attitude I once had. Compassion is what we are called upon to have when we understand that we are all the same. My mother and I were the same; neither of us was better than the other, but we both had the tremendous potential for Godliness.

It was the proper attitude. So that by the time my father died and my mother had invited another alcoholic to live with her, I did not hate her for her decision. I was disappointed, but I understood. And I did not have to justify her decision or take up for her against the onslaught of criticism and genuine concern from my siblings. By that time I understood what I could and could not change.

*   *   *

I have a girlfriend who always felt her siblings did not love and respect her. What has happened over the years that I've known her is that her vision of herself has almost become a self-fulfilling prophecy.

She is the next-to-the-oldest child in a family of eight. Looking at her, I have often considered what an ambiguous position that must be in a large family. She says no one respects her opinion or treats her as if she is the oldest.

I empathize with her, knowing how much attention and respect I command as the oldest and how little of that naturally falls on my sister Shelia, who is the next oldest.

My friend, though, is also timid, not at all sure of herself. It is as if she doesn't trust her own opinions, and so I wonder, too, how much of her family's reaction is to this. Or which came first? At any rate, their hesitancy to accept her advice or respect her judgment has created a chip on her shoulder. When she is dealing with her siblings, she becomes more and more defensive, certain they do not respect her or believe a word she says. Of course, the more defensive she becomes, the more they retreat from her.

They no longer offer the constructive criticism to her that they give to one another. They hesitate to make suggestions. One of her brothers, who seems to be a very argumentative person, knows that his sister is easily riled, and so when he wants to argue, he picks an argument with her. My friend wears her chip on her shoulder where anyone can see it, so she's an easy target.

Now, after years of watching, I see that my friend's belief about herself—that she is not respected by her siblings—is becoming true. It has reminded me again of how important it is to hold in our minds the vision of who we want to be. How important it is to see ourselves as we want others to see us.

If I had just walked into my friend's life I would believe her siblings are picking on her. But because our families have been close for so many years, I have been able to watch as she became who she thought she was and they began to treat her as she believed they would.

How will the dynamics change in that family? How can my friend become respected in the family? For one, she has to look at herself in relationship to her family and understand what is really going on. I believe she has to focus more on herself and not on what she thinks others think about her. After years, I finally saw the correlation between her family life and her life outside the family. She needs to make that connection, too.

She has been fired or asked to leave nearly every job she ever had, though she keeps each one about five years. After the last firing, she explained, "I didn't do something that nobody else did. They let other people get away with the same thing they fired me for."

In other words, people were picking on her again, treating her the same way her sisters and brothers did. This time, she was fired for always being late. Well, when I thought about it, my friend was late for every family gathering, too, often holding up an event, arriving late with a very necessary dish, setting off a chain of events that left everyone angry and inconvenienced. It was not the kind of behavior that wins anyone respect, inside or outside a family.

This time, I suggested, "Don't compare yourself to the worst people on your job. Whenever you do that, you know you have a problem. How about the best people? Were they always late, too?"

She was flustered. After all, I had always been her confidante and supporter. Yet when I thought about it, my friend never focused on herself or the possibility that she might have problems! She did not look at herself and did not accept constructive criticism from inside or outside the family. I know that the bottom line is she doesn't love herself enough to give her soul the care she gives to everyone else.

For years, I followed her lead on this journey, believing that it was her siblings and her employers who were against her. But I was sidetracked, too, by her charm, kindness, and poise. Now I am hoping she is up to the task of changing.

I told her recently, "You will know you are changing when you can hear your sisters criticize you—and you listen. You won't fight back. You listen, then hang up and think about what was said."

I know people who fret because they have no family. I don't pretend to understand what that feels like, but I know that you don't have to have blood relatives to create a family. You can make a family, if you want one.

At the age of forty I discovered that my father, the only man I have ever called Dad, was not my biological father. I have met my biological father once since that discovery. I had to decide, "Who is my real father?" I chose the man who raised me, the man whom I did not understand for many years, but who I know loved me and cared for me in the only way he knew how. I chose the man whose love I knew as opposed to the man whose love I had never known.

I am told that I have half-sisters and half-brothers and yet I chose not to meet them. I decided I have enough family. I have five sisters and a brother—and I would not think of my biological father's children as my siblings, regardless of our blood. I knew this in my heart. I was so satisfied with my family. And I think that was what made the difference. If we are satisfied with our love, we don't need to go searching for another family. That doesn't mean adoptive children should not want to meet their biological parents. I certainly wanted to meet mine. But it didn't matter to me whether or not there was a "family" relationship. I have a family.

The whole episode made me ask the question: What is a family? I was more sure than ever that we can make a family. Of course, my situation is not as challenging as some. But the question of family—who they are, how they fit into our lives, how we fit into theirs—must be sorted out if we are to be healthy enough to change.

At home, we learn how to interact with other human beings. Therefore, when our laboratory known as family is in disarray, what we learn can be very harmful to our existence. Before I changed my perception of love and realized my father really did love me, I desperately searched for male love in the arms of men who abused me. Because my friend refuses to consider that some of the criticism her family offers could be true, she will not delve into her psyche enough to know why she is so defensive. Therefore, she will never hear the warnings and advice offered to her on the job. Consequently, her career may never flourish.

When we leave home carrying suitcases of unresolved

family issues, we may find those very issues will manifest as problems outside of the family. We will create spiritual gridlock because of our refusal to take those moments to change.

It is never too late to step back and take a good look at that human lab we call family, at what happened to us there, at what good we can take with us, and what we might need to change before going on. It is up to us to nurture our roots, or to replant ourselves in conditions suitable to our growth.

Once we become our own caretakers, we choose the conditions: how much light, how much rain, how we will feed our spirits. That is what I did through therapy.

Strengthening our roots might mean weeding out the misconceptions we have about our family, or separating ourselves from the poisonous branches within our own family tree. Or, it may mean accepting with grace where we have been planted, knowing all the time that we have the power to grow stronger and taller as we reach for God's light.

5

If You Don't Have the Job You Want, Act Like You Love the Job You Have

WORK

◆

For too much of my life I worked at jobs I did not enjoy. In fact, I never considered that *joy* and *work* could be or should be synonymous. I worked only for money with no regard to pleasure, performing nonchallenging duties I could do without tiring my brain. I collected my paycheck and partied all weekend so I could forget how miserable I would be again on Monday.

Later, as my life changed and I began to concern myself with the quality of each moment, I had to face questions regarding work. What kind of work suited me? What kind of work would bring me joy?

Work is another laboratory where we consider our individual spiritual and psychological problems. On our jobs, we should discover what kind of work brings us joy and gives our lives meaning. We will also be presented opportunities to examine and conquer some of the same problems we face off the jobs, such as a lack of confidence or an inability to accept criticism.

I recall being proud of my first job at age fifteen, when I was a teacher's aide for a Head Start Program in my neighborhood of Glenarden, Maryland. It was a summer job, and not only was I thrilled to be earning money, but I also was happy because I was working with little children. My sense of pride came from feeling as though I was making a difference in their lives.

Then all too quickly, at age nineteen, I was the mother of a daughter, and there was no time to think about what kind of work I wanted to do or what kind of career I wanted. I had to work to earn money to pay for rent, food, and clothes. I learned new skills for the sole reason of earning more money. I went to school at night and on weekends to learn to type faster and to study shorthand and bookkeeping.

I moved to North Carolina, where I worked at a string of office jobs, as a Teletype operator, a bookkeeping clerk, a clerk-typist, and a secretary. On Fridays I beat a path to a juke joint, drank cheap liquor, and danced hard along with everybody else who hated their nine-to-fives. At other times I sat under a red light in someone's apartment, nodding with friends, high on heroin, emptying our heads of our misery.

For ten years, I worked on automatic pilot, filing, typing, and collecting my paycheck doing a string of office jobs I could have done with my eyes closed. I was working at the *Charlotte Observer* newspaper in Charlotte, North Carolina, when I realized I had to make a change in my work. I was so bored with my secretarial duties that I fell asleep typing letters, or sometimes I just drifted off into my daydreams.

I filed and refiled, arranged and rearranged, and one day when there was no more busywork to do, I told my boss I couldn't take it any longer. My days of being a secretary were over. He offered me a better title and more money, but I knew that in actuality, it only meant the same duties—just more of them.

But this was the first time I ever considered that maybe a job should be enjoyable. I was twenty-nine.

It was at home that I discovered I enjoyed writing; that it gave me joy and peace; that when I could not say something, could not speak of my anger or depression, I could write it down and feel healed—if only for a while. Yet I didn't think of writing as being a real profession. It was a whim, an art practiced by people whose magical lives I read about in magazines and books.

This is the problem with many of us. We have a talent or skill that we enjoy immensely, but we only think of it as a hobby, "a little something I do in my spare time." Yet, the truth may be that the "little something" is what we should be doing with most of our time because it is the work that will give us joy.

To keep myself on the right track, I used to keep on the

bulletin board over my desk at the *Washington Post* a quote from *The Prophet* by Kahlil Gibran. It said: "Work is love made visible."

I have a friend, Richard Koonce, who as part of his work as an employment consultant helps people find their life's work. Richard's approach to employment is a combination of practical and spiritual, a mixture I never considered until I met him.

"We work eleven thousand days of our life between ages twenty-one and sixty-five—more or less," he likes to point out. "So it is important that we find work that is meaningful. You know you have the right kind of work if you are energized by that work."

He helps people find work that fits their "talent, experience, and temperament," and he says we don't have to take a vow of poverty to follow our dreams.

"If we listen to the voice in ourselves, we know what we want to do," said Richard, whose advice can be found in his book, *Career Power. Twelve Winning Habits to Get You from Where You Are to Where You Want to Be.* (Amacon, 1994)

"I believe we are all born with certain talents, skills unknown to us but that are right in our hip pocket. It's up to us to mine the ore so we can realize our fortune."

Richard has often seen those difficult moments, when a person is laid off or a job ends, become a breakthrough to a more satisfying job. In other words, circumstances push us on when we would otherwise hesitate to change jobs.

"You have to learn to take responsibility for managing your careers, because your vision for yourself may go farther than anyone else (such as a boss) can imagine for you," he advises. "Develop what I call a healthy feistiness: Say, 'I will not let someone else dictate to me what I will do.'

"We all need to find passion in our work in order for us to be sustained," said Richard. "We have to know, too, that it is never too late to make a change."

*   *   *

Ironically, it was my secretarial work that led me to the work that would become my passion and joy. At the *Observer,* I stepped into a newsroom for the first time and saw that there were people who actually worked in an office and earned their living writing.

I had never consciously considered journalism as a profession until I saw real reporters at work with my own eyes. Sometimes you have to see something to make it a reality in your life. While some of us can see our dreams clearly in our imaginations, others have our visions clouded by such things as guilt, drugs, and lack of confidence. I believe God had to take me by the hand to lead me and show me in reality what I could not imagine.

Still, I almost left my secretarial job without opening my eyes to what was right before me. I was just two floors down from my dream come true, and I almost did not see it. Often, we are so miserable on our jobs we can't see the answers or opportunities that lie near us.

After I talked to my boss about my discontent with my secretarial job, he got me a job as a transcriber, working in the newsroom, which was my introduction to reporters. I worked part-time while I attended classes at a community college. Some months later, I began working in the newsroom as a research writer, and then I began writing small articles. When I heard about a summer journalism training program, I applied and was accepted. Upon graduation, I got my first job, as a reporter at the *Miami News* in Miami, Florida.

I was no longer bored. I felt challenged, exuberant, and joyful. I made more money and could afford a better place to live and to pay for my daughter's drama classes. But the biggest perk was that I had finally found a job that gave me joy.

I felt as I did when I was a young Head Start worker, that I was helping others with my work. I was able to encourage readers with my words and to write stories that had the power to change people's lives.

But finding joy in our work is a difficult state of being to hold on to, particularly in a culture that tells us that work is drudgery and that joy is something we buy at a resort or on a cruise. Our culture tells us, too, that our worth (both financially as well as our worth as human beings) is tied to how we earn our money and how much money we make.

*　　*　　*

While my new job as a reporter boosted my self-esteem, it could not instantly raise my esteem from rock bottom to the height where it needed to be. I still thought of myself as stupid, and one of the first problems this misconception caused was that it made me reluctant to ask questions I thought I should know the answer to. For instance, if I was interviewing a Catholic archbishop and he referred to some controversial incident in the Catholic church that I only knew about vaguely, I didn't ask him to "Please, refresh my memory" or say something like "I don't know all the details in the case, would you go over it for me, briefly."

No, I was too afraid that I might sound stupid. I was still the kid afraid to raise her hand in class for fear she might be wrong. I was still the young colored girl who thought she represented every member of her race each time she opened her mouth. So there I was in that human laboratory called "work," and, of course, the issues of self-confidence and self-esteem would crop up again.

Not asking the proper questions meant I was more likely to make mistakes. Instead of asking the person before me to answer the questions, I was left to search frantically through files of newspaper clips for the answer later. After a couple of serious mistakes, I was forced to change—or lose my job. I learned to ask any question, even though I still thought some of them were stupid ones.

Because I worked for white-owned papers, where the majority of the staff was also white, I was constantly questioning myself, too, about the points of view portrayed in the newspapers where I worked. Specifically, I wondered if I could work for an institution that seldom expressed my viewpoint in its paper. In other words, could I work for institutions that were often perceived as racist because of the way in which they portrayed blacks or their editorial views on issues important to black people?

On my very first job as a reporter—at the *Miami News*—I faced this question head-on. A black man who was an insurance executive and ex-marine was killed by some Miami police officers. At the trial, the officers were found not guilty. Part of the black community erupted in a riot, and when I went out as a reporter to cover it, I was seen as a traitor and an enemy by people on the street.

This was hard to swallow. I saw myself as being the same as the people who now hated me. Yet there was no time to talk to them. They were angry and hurt. I hurt, too, in some ways twice as much. I was in pain, suffering from the same injustices they suffered, but I was denied the opportunity to be consoled because my very own people now pushed me away rather than embracing me.

I suffered through those times. I questioned myself: was I a traitor? I asked myself: why am I working as a reporter? Why at a white-owned newspaper?

After the flames died down and the smoke faded from over the city, I resigned from the newspaper. I was needed at home in Washington, where my mother was straining to care for her own mother, who had suffered a stroke. But going to help my mother was just a legitimate reason to escape. I actually left because I did not know what to do with this occupation that was my joy and also, for the time being, the cause of so much pain.

In Washington I worked several temporary jobs while turning over in my head some other possibilities. I was working a temporary job as a secretary at a civil rights organization when I realized I could not shake my love for journalism and so I would have to return.

Meanwhile, I made friends easily on the temporary job, but I noticed that their reactions to my having been a reporter fell into two categories—those who didn't believe me (After all, why would a reporter work as a secretary?) and those who did but who said with their attitudes and often with words: "That's nice, darling, but you're a secretary now. So get over it and bring me a cup of coffee."

Ironically, a major service provided at the organization was to provide training for some people, find jobs for others, and to encourage everyone. So when I decided to pursue journalism again, I happily announced this to a couple of managers and co-workers. I'll never forget what one of the managers said. "Patrice, there are only two newspapers in this city. Do you know how many people want to work for them?" Then she walked away, as if there was nothing else to say on the subject.

The executive secretary who supervised me said, "Well, you can't always get what you want." Then she pointed out that the man who drove the organization's bus wanted to be a firefighter. "You see what he's doing?" She raised her eyebrows, as if I should respond. This time, I walked away.

Both women also noted that I did not have a college degree. "This is a city where everybody has credentials," the manager said.

For a few days, I believed them. Of course, I could not expect to find a reporter's job when there were only two major newspapers to choose from, lots of competition, and I had no college degree. Then one day, listening to those two women gossip about everybody on the job, it occurred to me that I was looking in the wrong place to receive encouragement.

I returned to prayer and to faith. I went on to get a job first at the *Washington Star* and later at the *Washington Post,* the two major papers in the city. Years later, when I was at the *Post,* I ran into one of the women who had tried to discourage me. This time she was praising me for some of the stories I had written for the *Post.* Did she remember what she had said to me years earlier? I doubt it. I believe cynicism and pessimism had become a natural part of her makeup. She probably thought she was helping me by giving me what she considered a dose of reality.

Perhaps she did not understand the power of the spoken word. Even after I got a job at the *Washington Star,* I heard her words about my lack of credentials echoing in my head. It was true that most of my journalist peers had college degrees. Therefore, I told myself, they had to be more qualified, and surely, they could do a better job.

With this message thundering in my head, I returned to my unwise practice of not asking questions I thought I should know the answers to. I was covering education in a suburban community of Washington, D.C. Just the thought of this assignment intimidated me. I had worked as a feature writer in Miami, which meant I studied and honed up on my writing skills. I studied fiction and good journalistic writing, trying to perfect a style. I did not give any attention to investigative skills, analyzing data, or any of the skills I would need as an education reporter.

Actually, I made the job harder than it was. I was imagining I had to have some pie-in-the-sky skills, when all I needed was common sense and to know who to ask for the information I did not know. But my own fear stopped me dead in my tracks, prohibited me from asking questions again, and made my lack of confidence grow until it threatened to consume me. With this attitude, I had problems. I missed points that should have been made and even some whole stories because I was too afraid to ask people at the board of education or the school system the information I felt I should know.

My probation period on the job was extended. I told myself it was happening because I really didn't want to work in a predominantly white suburb covering education; I wanted to work in the inner city writing about social issues. This was true, but it did not explain away my fears. Before I worked out that problem, the *Washington Star* closed. So I would have to return to this lesson again, somewhere else.

If we use our jobs to grow, even the work that does not bring us joy yet will help pave the way for the work of our dreams. At the *Washington Post* I later would return to my fears as a reporter. I had to learn that investigative reporting is not as difficult as I made it, that I could do it as well as anyone else—if only I asked for help when I needed it—and if I didn't allow my fears to stop me from learning. In fact, I learned to enjoy investigative reporting, though feature writing is still my greatest joy when working at a newspaper.

*   *   *

Joy should not be relegated to weekends. We *must* find joy in our work. When we do, we are rewarded, both personally and professionally.

I was reminded of this one rainy day when I had to catch two taxicabs, to and from work. I could hardly wait to get out of the first cab. The driver was surly and rude. But it was a pleasure to ride in the second car, which was immaculate. The driver of that cab was very pleasant, though he said very little. He greeted me with a joyful "good morning." When we reached my destination, he said, "Thank you for this trip"—and this was before I even tipped him! When I tipped him, he bid farewell with, "God bless you for this tip."

I don't have to tell you which driver got the largest tip. The second driver emanated joy, and I felt as though I was tipping him for more than a ride. Perhaps he would be a driver for only another day, or maybe for years. Maybe he was studying at night to be a lawyer. Maybe he had found his life's work. Who knows. There was no way of telling. All I knew, or cared to know, was that for the time when he was my taxi driver, he was joyful. I am sure his workdays zoom by fast and his tips are large.

On another day, I read an article in the *Post* about a school crossing guard who delighted the students, parents, and teachers who passed her each day. She was cheerful, helpful, and attentive. For nearly a decade, she became the friend of each person who passed. Sure, maybe they only spent a minute or two together each weekday, but she made them happy for the short time she was in their lives.

Even after her husband began to suffer with multiple sclerosis, the woman still came to do her job and she was still cheerful. When her husband could no longer stay at home alone she brought him with her, to sit in their decrepit van and wait until she stopped cars and waved people safely across the streets.

The article was about how they repaid her. The students, teachers, and parents raised $15,000 and bought her a van with special features for a handicapped person as well as a CB radio, television, and air-conditioning.

The mother of one former student said, "Patty makes roses out of dandelions. No matter how difficult her life is, she somehow makes time to brighten our day."

The story of Patty made me think of a favorite quote from a speech by Dr. Martin Luther King Jr. In the speech, made in Chicago during March of 1965, King spoke of how a person should seek to do this life's work as if God Almighty called him to do it. "If you can't be a pine on the top of a hill, be a scrub in the valley, but be the best little scrub on the side of the hill. Be a bush if you can't be a tree. If you can't be a highway, just be a trail. If you can't be the sun, be a star. For it isn't by size that you win or you fail. Be the best of whatever you are."

*   *   *

We are defined not by our occupation but by how well we do our work.

Before I knew this, I thought my sole success and source of professional respect from my peers would come at the *Post*. After working on the Metro section of the newspaper for about seven years, I expressed an interest in writing for the Style section or the *Magazine*. Those sections most often allowed opportunities to write different, more creative forms of feature stories. But I was rejected by both sections basically for the same reason: I did not write in a manner suitable for either.

I was gravely disappointed and angry. I thought that even though I didn't have the qualifications I was still a longtime employee, and the company should want to train me so that I could grow professionally. They owed me, I reasoned.

I sulked, physically and mentally. I no longer liked my job or the company. Everything was wrong. I got up in the morning and dreaded walking into that newsroom. I felt as though I had outgrown the job I had. It had become boring and joyless.

I knew I had to do something to keep myself from going crazy, so I took a class, something I would enjoy: creative writing. Then I joined a group of women writers who met regularly to critique one another's writings and to talk and support one another. The feedback I got was encouraging. I could write! I wasn't as bad as I had begun to believe, after digesting the rejection I received at work.

I had to remember who I really was.

Basically, I was looking for joy outside of my job because I could not find it at work. I applied for entry into a prestigious artists colony in New Hampshire and was accepted based on my writing and recommendations. I applied for a creative writing class taught by author Gloria Naylor and was accepted. All of this boosted my self-esteem. I was also happy on the job again because I had found joy in my work—writing—even if it wasn't at my place of employment.

But it also taught me that it was important to know myself. After a string of successes, I could still get rejected with the next application, so my fate must not be left up to the whim of the next critic.

* * *

We do not know where our success will come from. Sometimes we limit ourselves by believing it can only come from one place. I thought I had to be successful at the *Post*, and the only way that success could happen was if I got a different job that allowed me to write in a different way. I forgot that there were many other forms of writing that had nothing to do with newspapers. I had forgotten that before I fell into journalism I had dreamed of becoming an author and playwright.

Once I accepted that success could come—even if it did not happen at the *Post,* my vision expanded and doors opened. But I had to be prepared. I studied, took classes, and read. A friend became a literary agent and insisted I write a book. She told me what books to buy to teach myself how to write a book proposal, and I went to classes to prepare myself.

Before long, I had a book proposal and ten publishers

interested in publishing it. Then I had another career as an author and public speaker as well as my job as a reporter. Suddenly, too, it did not matter to me whether or not I could write for the *Magazine* or Style. The world was my employer. My possibility for success was limitless!

I used to think that as a competitive *Washington Post* reporter my main goal on the job should be to get stories on page one. Still, I always understood that reporting entailed intruding into people's lives, and I was careful not to tamper with much. Yet, the front page was never far from my mind.

But we can't leave our religion at home when we go to work. I could not swap my respect for others for the opportunity to be on page one. I had to remember my spirituality, morals, values, and sense of fairness.

Now I seldom think of the front page. I pray to leave a person's life better than I found it, I pray to learn and to teach and to use each story as an opportunity to make the world better.

But before I learned this lesson I competed with another reporter as we both worked on the follow-up story about a house fire. From what neighbors said, there were about a dozen men and a woman in the house, all of them believed to be alcoholics. Several people perished in the fire, including the woman, but the neighbors knew the woman better than the men, since she had been around the neighborhood a long time, while the men were new immigrants from El Salvador.

The story we wrote reflected what the neighbors said about the woman. They painted her as a loud, cursing vagrant who may have prostituted for the price of a bottle of wine. I also met the woman's distraught brother and sister, her mother and her child, a toddler raised by the family. The dead woman, the family said, had strayed from her middle-class upbringing and high school honor roll student image. She had a drinking problem, but they loved her and had hoped she would return. The story we wrote mentioned the family but focused more on what the neighbors said about the woman.

The first call I got after the paper came out the next day was from a male friend whose opinions I respected. He said, facetiously, "Oh, so now you're dogging dead people. Wasn't it enough that the woman was killed in the fire? Did you have to drag her memory through the dirt?" The next call was from the woman's aunt, who wailed with pain between her stabbing accusations. "You killed her again! This article is all her child will have to remember his mother. Do you think we will ever let him read it?"

Mostly, I listened. But as so often is the case, I knew I had done wrong before anyone had said a word to me. The night after I finished the story and left work, I began having doubts. What had happened to me? I think I lost my own conscience by getting hyped up by the competition, by wanting to look smart to my co-worker. I lost my focus, my religion, my definition of myself.

It was another lesson at work that I would never forget.

∗   ∗   ∗

Not everyone will earn millions in a lifetime or become a household name, identified by their chosen field of work.

Some of us will flip hamburgers, toss pizzas, clean toilets, wait on tables, and shovel dirt. All of these jobs are necessary and worthy.

Try to imagine our world without any of these. Jobs exist because we need the services and products they provide. We should then vow to be kind and patient with the person working at Burger King. Appreciate how sanitary the bathrooms are in our offices. Smile at the work crews along the road.

They are as valuable as the doctors, lawyers, football players, and scientists. If only they could all be paid what they are worth.

Who decides worth? Of course, there is a complex economic rule that tries to explain why certain people receive the salaries they do in our system of capitalism. So for now, we are stuck in this culture, which worships materialism and titles. Accepting this, then we must each decide our own worth. A paycheck cannot tell us what our value is on this earth.

Know your own worth and you're a step closer to finding joy in your work.

*　　*　　*

One day I was standing in line on a downtown Washington corner a few blocks from the White House, waiting to buy a burrito from a vendor when I heard a young lady in line remark that the vendor "used to be a lawyer at the law firm where I work." I was intrigued. I had noticed when the vending cart first appeared on the corner, and I had watched as the line grew longer and longer at each lunchtime. Curiosity and the desire for a meatless lunch pushed me to join the line. Boy, was I rewarded! The burrito was great—so fresh and delicious—and the vendor was so pleasant, I returned almost daily for several weeks.

One evening I spent a couple of hours talking to the vendor, whose story and wisdom on the subject of work bears repeating.

James F. Tiu was twenty-nine when I met him, but mentally and spiritually he was much older. He grew up in Wheeling, West Virginia, where his father is a physician and his mother is a nurse.

"Growing up, I worked at my father's clinic," said James. "All of my father's friends and my role models seemed to be medical professionals."

No one pushed James into the profession, but he chose to follow in his parents' footsteps, entering Xavier University in Cincinnati, Ohio, in 1983. He picked his career the way most of us do, "because it was what I knew," he explained. But by his sophomore year, he knew he did not want to be a doctor. He was a good student, but he admits he was not willing to make the sacrifices to study and do the work he needed to get into medical school.

Then in the summer between his junior and senior year, James had an experience that would forever remain important in his life: he went to work at the Keebler Bakery, packing cookies.

"It was a union factory position, strictly blue-collar," said James. "I wore an apron and hair net, and hit the clock. It was a very mundane job in a rigid environment.

Many of the jobs were physically repetitive and uncomfortable. But I learned a lot about patience and endurance—and about what I didn't want to do with my life."

The job paid $11.50 an hour, which was a good salary for many and very good for someone in college, so James continued to work at the cookie factory until graduation.

"That taught me I could—if I wanted to—always return to a very humble way of making a living," said James.

By this time he had decided he wanted to become a lawyer. He entered the University of Cincinnati in the fall of 1988 and excelled there.

"I never had a burning desire to go to law school, but it appeared a better alternative than spending the next twenty years in a cookie factory," James noted.

He attracted the attention of a Washington, D.C., law firm and managed to garner a job there for two summers. Then after graduation in the fall of 1991, he became the envy of his peers by going to work at the firm, which handled government contracts.

In his new job, James traveled, reviewing documents for various cases. He remembers, "It was repetitive. I had a box of documents to go through by the end of the day. In many ways it reminded me of the cookie factory.

"The underlined similarity was that I knew after two and a half years that I had come up against something that I was not going to be satisfied with doing all of my life. I always felt a person should have a calling—and should listen to their calling. I knew myself that it was highly unlikely that my calling was going to be a job that someone else had envisioned for me. It was much more likely that the job that was going to be satisfying to me would be one that I would create myself."

When trying to decide what his life's work would be, James considered what he had done so far.

"I had an evolving life of service that began in childhood. My parents were always serving others. Whenever I went home for the Thanksgiving and Christmas holidays, my family went to shelters for the homeless to distribute meals.

"I went to a Catholic high school and a Jesuit university, and service to others was emphasized at both. As I became older, I took on more and more volunteer opportunities to serve others. . . . I realized I wanted to really help people, to serve them. I was never bored when I felt I was truly serving someone. How could you be bored when you got a sense of satisfaction from working for more than money, from making someone's life better."

In the back of his mind, there was brewing an idea that combined his love for burritos and the kind of vending cart he frequented to buy cappuccino. But first he tried one more time to find the right job. For six months, he applied to jobs at other firms, thinking a minor adjustment would suit him.

He did not pray for more pay or more prestige. "I prayed very hard that I would find something that would satisfy me," said James.

The idea of a vending cart that sells burritos was taking prominence in his mind. He dreamed of it. He thought of it in between interviews.

"If I examined my life very honestly, from a very early age I knew someday in the future I wanted to own my own business. To me, running a small start-up business was about as exciting an adventure as one could undertake. I knew from my own experiences that I had the capacity to change myself from doing something that was one type of work to doing another—if I had to."

Soon there was no denying what he really wanted. He still had student loans, very little money, and a good-paying job that was the envy of many young law associates. Yet he knew it was time to try to turn his dream into reality.

He guarded the dream, telling few people, protecting himself against the naysayers. He quit his job and went to work the next day as a waiter at a nearby sports bar. Over the next four months, he scraped together some funds, found some investors and business partners, and incorporated the business.

He didn't have any equipment or any idea how to run a street vending cart. But his faith made doors open. Three weeks after he left the firm, the woman who ran the cappuccino cart he frequented let him operate the cart for her three hours a day so she could run errands.

By the time I stood in line to buy burritos from James he had been in business on the downtown corner surrounded by shops, law firms, and banks for a year.

"I have not had one regret," James told me. "There's

no greater joy than knowing you're doing each day what you were born to do."

He is serving people—even if it doesn't seem on the surface to be the kind of service he grew up rendering in his father's clinic or at the shelters for the homeless.

As for the future, James said, "I could tell you that my goal is to open a storefront and increase business five times. But that will happen if God intends it. If this business serves its customers and treats its suppliers and other competitors, vendors, and anyone else involved the same way we want to be treated, then I think a natural result will be that business is going to grow.

"I was blessed with knowing I wanted to serve others, and I had a general sense that if I followed where my heart was taking me, I would be okay. I knew I could not live with myself if I had a good idea and didn't give it a try. You can't know every factor."

James didn't know if people would stand in line outside to buy burritos, since no one else in Washington was selling them from vending carts.

"The day I opened up the awning on my cart, my hands were shaking so bad. Here I was ready to face my friends, people I didn't know, the partners at the firm. And I was doing it alone.

"I was praying every single moment that disaster would not strike," he recalled. "But I don't believe we are meant to live our lives in fear. We human beings worry about far too many things."

James was determined not to give in to fear. His reward

was joy, a continuous flow of it that he still feels each day he rolls open the awning on his burrito cart.

*   *   *

Know that you are exactly where you should be, that there is a reason you are working at the job where you work today. Perhaps, like James when he was at the cookie factory, your job is helping you discover your strengths, your likes and dislikes, lessons you might use to find your life's work.

In fact, James credits the law firm with teaching him what work was not suitable for him, but most of all for bringing him to Washington, where he could see and admire the cappuccino vending cart on the corner near his office.

"I was offered a tremendous opportunity to perform at a law firm—and it was without the least bit of animosity that I left," said James. "A large number of my customers are from the firm. I care about them and their business."

So many of us remain on jobs we hate until we transfer our anger to our co-workers and most often to our bosses. By the time we leave, we believe we hate the people we worked with and for.

*   *   *

Until you find your passion, be joyful in the job you have, so that joy might multiply and bring to you your good while leading you to the work you were born to do. Sometimes we have to stay in a holding pattern—where we learn—before we move on to the next level. The next level may be a new job at a different place of employment, a new job at the place where we now work, a totally different occupation, or the same job with a new attitude. There are an infinite number of possibilities. It's up to us.

We spend too many hours on the job to work only for money. We spend the cash, and then what do we have? What our work gives us should be everlasting, something that cannot be spent.

When I went on my book tour after the publication of the paperback version of *Laughing in the Dark,* I left home with trepidation. I did not want to catch two and three planes on some days, catch small commuter flights that scared the heck out of me, sleep in beds that were not my own, leave my family, or leave mild fall days for frozen winter weather.

A week after I embarked on my journey, my daughter called me at one of the hotels where I stayed in the Midwest. "Mom, how is the tour?" she asked, and I excitedly rattled off one detail after another for the next forty-five minutes. We hung up and she called right back. "Mom," she said, "we talked for forty-five minutes and you never told me how the book sales were going."

I told her about the people I had met. About the waiter in Milwaukee who was raising two daughters alone since his wife's death five years earlier. I told her how I whispered to him, "I don't think people really die," and how he grinned, leaned over my table, and whispered back, "I don't think so either. I tell my daughters all the time that she is with us. I know I have seen things she had to do." We talked about angels and spirits throughout my dinner. I told my daughter about the Thai cab driver who became my private driver after showing me papers from his lawyer and telling me the story of how he had come to Dallas to find the daughter his ex-wife gave up for adoption without his knowledge. I told my daughter about the millionaire restaurant owner and psychic who could touch people and know their lives; the escort whose thirteen-year-old son had died six months earlier and what she had learned from his death.

On my daughter's second call, I laughed and said, "I forgot about the book sales. You see, my publisher thinks he is sending me out here to sell books. But I think God is sending me out here to meet these people."

I returned from the tour exhausted but also renewed. I had met people in twelve different cities who made me hopeful about us human beings. They were people who believed in prayer, angels, spiritualism, and God. They were people all trying to make sense of this life, looking beyond what their eyes could see.

When you try to find the joy in your work, joy finds you.

*   *   *

Whenever I think about the worth of a job, I remember the man from the Prince George's County Hospice who came to wash my mother's body.

My mother died in her bedroom just as she wanted. Three weeks after the doctor discovered that the cancer had spread to her liver, she closed her eyes, went into a coma, and died as I sat next to her, cheering her to go on and be with God and thanking her for my life. It was Thanksgiving Day 1994.

Needless to say, it was an emotional time. But just as my mother had hoped, all of the family—her children and grandchildren—were able to pass through her room to say their good-byes. Before we had finished, the man from the hospice arrived. We had called the organization to tell them Mamma had passed. We knew someone would come, but we could not remember what would happen next.

Shortly after the man arrived, he asked, gently, that we leave the room. "I want to clean her up for you," he said. He spoke the words softly, as if they were magic. He said it as if it was his pleasure to do this for us.

Fifteen minutes later when we entered the room, we found the saliva that had caked at her mouth had been removed. Her lips were soft and clean again. Her skin was lotioned and smelled sweet, the way she liked it. She looked dignified. Pretty. Somehow, even happy.

How much did they pay this man for cleaning my mother's body? They could not possibly pay him enough. I was awestruck, even dumbfounded, considering what he had done. He told us he was going to have Thanksgiving dinner with his mother. And yet, before he did, he bathed my mother's body.

When he left, I knew that money is only an artificial means of expressing the worth of a job.

Money alone cannot pay us for the work we do.

6

The First Person

◆

You will not know love until you love yourself. Until then you may think that what exists between you and a spouse or boyfriend—even between a child and a parent—is love, but what you often have is admiration, respect, obsession, desperation, neediness, or some other feeling substituting as love.

I know. For years, I loved everyone—my daughter, my parents and siblings, my boyfriends and husbands—everyone, except me. I believed it would be selfish, egotistical, even sinful for me to focus on loving myself.

Now I think of it in this way: I am created in the image of God. If someone raises a hand against me, they strike God. If someone verbally abuses me, they curse God. Allowing yourself to be mistreated is disrespecting God. I would not disrespect or mistreat one creation of God, so why would I allow anyone else to do the same?

I'm convinced one of the reasons people find themselves unloved is because they do not see God in them-selves. They believe God is distant, in the sky, a person you see when you die. But we are told in many ways and in many writings that we are created in the image of God. In other words, we are God-like, at least when we are at our best. During our creation, a piece of God was planted in each of us. Love of self is the water and the sunshine that helps the Godliness within us to grow.

I constantly remind myself: if God is in us and we are God-like, then to dislike yourself is to hate God. To love yourself is to honor that which God has created.

To love yourself is to love God.

* * *

My journey to this point, from self-hatred to self-love, has been long and bumpy. Once I dated a man on my job who was dating another woman at the same time he dated me—and that woman worked with us, also. I could look right across the room into her eyes. Did I know he was dat-ing her, too? I think in the back of my mind, where I was in serious denial, I knew. But I was desperate for his love. For any love from any man. So I ignored my suspicions. I loved "love" more than I loved myself.

One day, I woke up and actually prayed, "God, let me see the truth." I went over to the guy's house and spent the night, then got up that morning and left early to go to teach a writing class. But the class time had been changed, so I doubled back to my boyfriend's house. In the car, I prayed again: "God, let me see the truth today." I started shaking almost uncontrollably. Holding the steering wheel as steady as I could, I drove on. I knew I was headed toward truth—and pain. I thought of turning around, but I drove faster.

When I returned to his house about an hour after I had left I found the other woman's car parked out front. I knocked on the door, but he refused to open the door. Later, he would reiterate that they were just friends and tell me that she had come over for breakfast. Of course, he scolded me for returning unannounced.

God had laid out the truth for me to see. But the truth hurt so much that I still tried to deny it. No one wants to feel like a sucker, rejected and unloved. I was feeling all of these things. So I called the other woman and asked, "Are you two still dating?" I must have sounded like I had lost my mind. I would understand later, when I had come to my senses, that if I had to call someone up and ask them about their relationship with my boyfriend, then I already had a problem, regardless of how the person answered the question.

The woman refused to talk to me but told me instead to ask him. I could tell she was startled—and hurt, too. In her voice, I heard myself. We were united by our lack of love for ourselves. And it was this lack that attracted the three of us to each other. We all had lessons to learn.

God had told me the truth, whether I wanted to hear it or not. My prayer had been answered. That woman's voice, the pain and discomfort in it, scared me. The next call I made was to a friend, asking her to refer me to a therapist. If I could be duped like this, after all the horrible relationships I had experienced, if I still did not love myself enough to avoid this kind of situation, I wanted help! I wanted someone to help me so I could love every crevice of my body, every flaw and fault. I wanted to heal myself with my own love. I was tired.

We are taught to deny our "self" in so many ways. Far too many men learn to work—not for joy—but for the family. And far too many women learn to care for others and put themselves last. And while there is some value in these thoughts, a man must eventually find joy in his work if he is to live a healthy life and be of benefit to his family and himself. And a woman must honor the God in herself, nurture herself, and use her healing talents on her own self if she is to be healthy, too.

When I speak to women's groups I often cite the following almost universal practice as an example of our denial of self. When we women cook, for instance when we fry chicken, and it is time to serve our families, we generally give the best, juiciest, fattest pieces to the men, then we may give the next best piece to ourselves. Or we may give the next best piece to our children, particularly if one child is a son. Then, when the choice servings are gone, we will take what is left for ourselves.

I did this for years. Then I began to wonder: do men do that when they serve? Do they give the best piece to the woman? Or do they figure because they are the male, perhaps the largest, physically, and the head of the house, they deserve or should by right have the best piece? I tell women, "It is all right to give away the best piece *some-*

times, if you are doing it because you believe the person deserves it that week. Perhaps, your husband has been particularly kind or patient and you want to encourage him.

"But I know that I fell into the practice of doling out the best because somehow that was what I was taught, that was the silent legacy passed on to me by my mamma and society. No one verbally told me, 'Give the best piece of chicken to the man.' But in so many silent ways, we pass along this message to our girls. Even in the serving of food, we deny our self and treat our own spirit as if it is less than the spirit of others."

*   *   *

Because I am a woman, I have given more thought to the ways in which women express their self-hatred or lack of love for themselves.

In *Laughing in the Dark* I wrote of a girlfriend's death and of how other friends told me she had stayed in a troubled marriage until it beat her down. It was the marriage and not her illness that killed her, they reasoned. The illness was simply the medical manifestation of it, they said. What added to a burden that became too heavy to carry was the way in which she suffered silently—and to some degree, the lack of love she had for herself.

Now when I think of her I also think of the words I wrote about her death. As I sat at my computer, I relived the pain and suffering I felt, and I tried to capture the exact timbre of my sorrow in words. I wrote: "When I considered her life, I felt her pain. It was a woman thing, I told myself. We women die in so many ways. Before a medical examiner proclaims us dead, we give our lives away."

After my mother died of breast cancer, I contemplated for days the ways in which she had denied herself joy even greater than the juiciest piece of chicken. She had remained married to my father, though they slept in separate rooms and though she was terribly unhappy. My mother was an emotional woman who loved to dish out kisses and hugs, and my father was a distant man uncomfortable with expressions of love. He held back so much that his silence created a gulf between them, and the silence turned to something that at times resembled hatred.

After my father died and my siblings and I had spent some time grieving, we sighed with some comfort knowing mother would finally be free of her old life. We thought one day she might find a man who loved her the way she begged to be loved and she would live happily ever after. Instead, she began to date an abusive alcoholic man who treated her worse than my father had.

When she detected her cancer, it was a huge lump on her right breast. A year after a mastectomy a doctor discovered the cancer was in her liver. Less than a month later, my mother was dead.

While I was still numb with shock, I wondered: did my mother ever in her life have anyone who thought enough of her to caress her breasts? To notice every scar or bruise on her, or the changes in her body? Did she love herself enough to stare at her curves and sags in the mirror? To smile, as I do, at the way age changes us? Did she rub her own hands slowly and gently across the body God created as a vessel for her spirit?

I know that lack of love for yourself helps determine choices you make and that some of those choices can affect your health. In my midtwenties, I chose to love a man who verbally and physically abused me. I married John because I always searched for love outside of myself, and therefore, I hunted desperately for a man.

A year after I had married him, I was so stressed out that one morning I woke up to find I literally could not push myself up out of bed. I was paralyzed. John had to dress me and carry me to the hospital, where doctors ran all kinds of emergency tests on me. Eventually, a doctor came to whisper to me that he believed my problem was caused by stress. My muscles, he said, were wound so tight they could not move. I was having muscle spasms, uncontrollable flinches inside my body.

I thought he was lying. I thought the idea that illnesses can be caused by our state of mind was a fantasy used on television soap operas. I had never heard of anyone really getting sick from the life they lived—at least not suffering from something like paralysis. People I knew got stabbed or shot or died of an overdose of drugs. No one died because loving someone was killing them.

When I left John, he had hit me only once. But he had abused me verbally and with his actions in a million different ways. And I had been silent. Because I did not understand my own worth, I did not understand that I deserved a better life—and that it could be mine if only I claimed it.

One of my dearest friends has been living through hell recently because she discovered her husband has been having an affair and that he and his girlfriend had a child. She has an opportunity for a moment of grace, a chance to learn some profound lessons. But so far, she has refused to learn.

During a confrontation with him, he roughed her up, slamming her against a wall and choking her nearly unconscious. This was the first time he had physically abused her, but what she had always managed to overlook was the many times he had verbally abused her. All of her friends and her family had heard it—how he overlooked her opinions, how he demanded she agree with him, how he always had to be right.

But she remains deaf. Now she partially blames herself for his affair.

"I was not giving him the attention I used to. I lost my job and my parents died. I was depressed." She cited other reasons, too, for his behavior.

"It does not matter," I said. "If you were cheating on him, having sex with men right in your house under his nose, that still doesn't mean he has to have an affair. That was his choice. There were other options: he could have left. He could have discussed the problem with you. He could have suggested counseling for the two of you."

The real problem—what is actually stopping my friend from seeing clearly—is her lack of love for herself. She is so focused on her husband—on his needs, on what he has said was the problem. She never stopped giving him attention. Her problem is that she gave him *all* of the attention. She never got to know herself. And she still will not focus on her needs.

As far as I could see, she had never changed—from the day she got married to the day she discovered her husband was cheating. It was her insecurities, her willingness to put him first—even before herself—that had attracted him, whether he realized it or not. He is a very insecure man, a man who does not like himself, so he creates a myth about who he is. He tells people he earns more money than he actually does. He spends money he can't really afford to spend. Deep inside, he is afraid that he is nothing, and he thinks his myths and money will make him something. He does not understand that being created by God makes us all someone. That being created by God makes being valueless impossible. But a man like him needs a woman like my friend. In fact, when his insecurities grew, he needed two women like my friend.

I have no doubt the other woman is just like my friend, equally as desperate, lacking just as much self-love.

When we don't love ourselves enough, we do not take the time to know ourselves, to define who we are and what we want. My friend was always focusing on the man in her life. To satisfy his lack of self-love her husband was also busy looking outside himself, too, though in a different way.

* * *

For years, I did whatever a man wanted me to do. I wore my hair in styles I thought would please the man I was with. I wore clothes I didn't even like. I remember friends walking up to me and saying, "Patrice, this isn't you," pointing to some latest hairstyle I was wearing or my most recent change in dress. They were right. Generally, I had changed my style to suit a man. How silly it all seems now. But at the time, like my friend, I was afraid to change. Afraid to put my desires before someone else's for fear they might leave me.

Being with a man meant everything. I warn women now: desperation has an odor to it. CK, Chanel, and Red can't cover it up. And a man instinctively knows the smell.

Desperation, which is only a lack of self-love, makes us settle for less than what we really want. Desperation in women also attracts a certain kind of man, a man who wants a woman he does not have to be responsible to or work hard to satisfy. In other words, he does not have to do the difficult work involved in growing spiritually—or changing.

Loving yourself means you are working on making yourself lovable. This does not mean fitting into someone else's notion of lovable. No, if you make yourself lovable while there is no one around, no mate or girlfriend or boyfriend, partner or spouse, then you are making yourself lovable for you—and for God. Then you are reaching the purest form of love, and you will attract someone who recognizes goodness or godliness.

If you mold yourself into what another human being

wants, you will always be at the whim and beck of that person. When that person changes their demands or their definition of what they want, even if it is not done viciously but because they, too, are confused, you are left floundering in the body of an imposter. A fake to yourself. If you create yourself after godliness, you will never be an imposter.

This doesn't guarantee that the person you love won't leave. But if they leave, you are left with someone else you love: yourself. While that may not seem like much of a comfort in the beginning, when you are feeling rejected or mourning the loss of the relationship, eventually your love for yourself, which is God at work, will help to heal you.

* * *

I am still traveling the road toward self-love. Some days I love myself unabashedly. On other days, I double back to the signpost labeled "self-love"—though never retreating as far back as I have in the past. On those days, I deny myself a million times to satisfy everyone else—my husband, my daughter, my stepdaughter, my siblings.

But I have come a mighty long way from being the girl in elementary school who hated herself because she had two big front teeth that the kids in school teased her about. Often, we don't realize the harm done to our children by school yard taunts. As parents, we have to question our children so we can learn what is harming them and then we have to do damage control.

Maybe a trip to the orthodontist would have helped me. But my mother told me a story about the one time she took me to an orthodontist. The dentist was white, and Mom found we were the only blacks in the office. After hours of sitting and being passed over, the receptionist finally called my name. Mamma said the doctor was so nasty to me that she ran from the office in tears, vowing never to return.

By the time she recounted the story to me I was over forty and not very sympathetic—at first. I kept thinking: this was not the only orthodontist in the world. Why didn't we go to another one?

There is some truth to my question, but there are other factors to consider, too. Who knows what might have happened if I had gotten braces and had my teeth straightened? Why worry or try to second-guess the past. Often we mistakenly think that by correcting something we consider a physical flaw, we will love ourselves. But I am reminded of a woman I once met in a writing class. She had been terribly overweight, once weighing some 300 pounds. She had her mouth wired so that she could not eat. After months of existing on liquid foods, she was a slim, svelte 125 pounds. She was a pretty woman, too, attracting a lot of attention from men for the first time in her life. Still, she was troubled. She hated herself. In her mind, she was still overweight. After years of being snubbed, mistreated, and taunted because of her extra pounds, she could not trust the affection and admiration of others, and she still could not love herself.

As I write this, I am wearing braces, trying to fix those protruding upper teeth that kept me from smiling in photos throughout elementary, junior high, and high school. But unlike that woman in my writing class, who still carried her weight in the form of self-hatred, I learned to love myself while I still had protruding teeth. I love myself so much I nearly chose to forget the braces. I am sure that regardless of how my teeth turn out, I will be fine.

*   *   *

We think we can hide our self-hatred; we may not realize it is there, but those with spiritual vision will see it nevertheless.

After I was raped, I began to walk with my shoulders rounded. I sank down into my waist with my chest caving inward. I became small and wished for invisibility. I had to live a lot of lessons to feel proud and loved again, to raise my shoulders and elongate my neck, to stretch from my center. When you walk regally, you breathe better, and that must affect our health, the very way in which our blood flows and purifies our organs.

Occasionally, in the grocery store line I will look at someone standing nearby and I immediately see their pain. I know the sunken posture that tries to pull away from the world. I know the droopy head that says "I am not loved." Other people recognize it, too, and there are those who—perhaps without realizing it themselves—are drawn to people who hate themselves, because next to them they feel powerful or in control. They prey on the weak, whether deliberately or subconsciously, because of their own inadequacies.

I can list a string of people I attracted when I was at the

peak of self-hatred: a man I dated who beat and raped me; a female hustler who stole from me; another date who never gave me anything but cocaine; a boss who gave me his girl-friend's work to do along with my own.

I gave them what they wanted, often denying myself. I was like my friend's husband, afraid that I was nothing. I needed people in my life to prove to myself that I was loved. In actuality, they were people who had no real love for me. Our relationships were based on a bond as invisible as air.

Besides thinking that I always had to give (beyond my own comfort) to establish and maintain friendships, I also suffered another misconception I find in many people. I thought that the only way to be Christian or godly was to open up my house, to give the shirt off my back, to give my last crumb of food to anybody who wanted it or asked.

I often find people confused about the messages of Christianity or more specifically, how to fit those principles into everyday life. We need to teach our children that it is God-like also to say, "No." To understand that the help requested may not be the help needed. That it is not selfish to consider your own needs, too.

I thought I had to be nice to everyone. It was my Christian duty. And what was nice? It was giving even when I did not want to, even when I did not have, even when my child and I suffered. Perhaps the most harmful part of my giving, though, was that I gave to feel Godly. Without the giving, I did not feel worthy or God-like. I needed to understand that I was already Godly, that the Creator made it so, and that I was therefore free to give in His name, not for the selfish reason of making myself feel good, or to have a friend.

We need to teach our children that we are connected to God. I believe this concept should be taught in school, that it is in fact essential to living. Not everyone has to learn it or listen, but I hope some will, that's all you need. Then we would not have children who grow up feeling loveless, helpless, fearful, or hopeless. We would not have children who grow up to kill another child over a $250 jacket. Our children would understand that to kill your fellow man over a material item is to kill God.

*   *   *

To love ourselves, we must forgive ourselves. Some of us easily forgive everyone else, but we forget to forgive ourselves, forget that we need to be forgiven also. We carry guilt around like shackles, dragging our past into our futures. Then we wonder why we don't respond quickly when we are being mistreated or disrespected. Those shackles are dragging us down! It's hard to flee—or exit—when there are shackles around your ankles.

Only after therapy did I forgive myself. I couldn't flee that cheating, two-timing man because I was trying to run with shackles of the past still hanging on my body. Forgive yourself! Give yourself permission to make another mistake. But learn from each mistake. Always take time out of each day, before you go to bed, to consider all that happened to you that day. Go over the good and the bad. Pat yourself on the back mentally for the good. Your spirit, courage, and wisdom can grow from these, they expand up to meet the future. Ponder the mistakes for what they are: moments in which you were given a chance to learn so that you will recognize the problem or challenge should it come your way again. Then, forget the past.

*   *   *

It is not always easy to love yourself in a world that encourages you to believe you are like fast food, replaceable and not very valuable. We have to be on our toes daily to overcome the negative messages we receive about who we are and about our worth. When I listen to some rap music, I cry for the poor young girls already suffering low self-esteem who must now deal with young men hyped on songs that encourage them to think of young women as "hos" and "bitches," people to freak and not love. And I don't care that the rappers say they are only talking about specific women. Those young girls, struggling with trying to love themselves, don't know that. That is why it is so very important that we be responsible for the messages we send out into the universe and the harm our careless words can cause!

As a woman, I know that my life is devalued in an infinite number of ways by laws, commercials, and magazines. This devaluing becomes a part of our thought process and we remember it, if not consciously then subconsciously, as we make decisions such as whether or not to demand a man use a condom when we have sex. If everything we learn says that as women the most important reason for living is to please a man or to have a man—or that we are only of value when we are with a partner—we are more likely to make any sacrifice necessary—even risking our health—to have love.

If we are gay or bisexual, we are told that we are abominations, sinners, unloved by God, and therefore, we spend energy and worry each day of our lives trying to be accepted and loved. I have seen people struggle and suffer greatly because of this, and I have always encouraged them to know that God loves them just as they are. It has always been my belief, anyway, that people are born in more sexual varieties than we acknowledge, that we will one day know the truth. Meanwhile, I cannot understand why love and sex become sins simply because they are between people of the same sex.

In our system of capitalism, where the emphasis is on money, we mistakenly believe our salaries reflect our worth. We hate ourselves because we don't earn more money or we don't hold certain kinds of job. As a black person, I had to learn to love myself in a society that honors whiteness and views people of color as less. I have watched as young white people deal with their own self-hatred, trying to decipher how much historical guilt to accept—if any—and how to be proud of their heritage, too.

We are all trying to find our way back to love, or in other words, back to God. Back to the beginning, when we were one with God and knew that we were perfect— whether we are gay, black, female, or poor.

*   *   *

Don't forget to love your body. It serves you well here on this earth, providing a home for your spirit. Check on it.

Study it. Get to know it. Some of us have more flesh than others. There really is just more of it to love.

You are the keeper of your body. God has entrusted you with its care. Don't destroy it with drugs or alcohol—or with more subtle killers such as silence. When someone hurts you, speak up. When someone makes a decision that causes you harm, let them know. Walk away, if necessary.

Don't dwell on past mistakes. Fill your time instead with thoughts of self-love. When you are going through a crisis that tugs at your foundation of self-love, remember better days—and know that this too will pass. God gives us those good days, the times when we have successes, so that we can remember what we are like when we are at our best.

We have all had successes, but we often overlook them because we hate ourselves so. Also, we may have too narrow a definition of success. Remember the good you have done for your children or a parent or friend. Remember answering questions correctly in class, getting a high score on a test. Remember that people always ask you about your houseplants because for some reason nature responds brilliantly to your care. Remember the days you were able to refrain from using drugs or any other crutches.

Remember those moments of grace, when you tapped into that unlimited God power that is available whenever you want it, and there will be no room in your head for negative thoughts about yourself.

*　　*　　*

I had to forgive myself for being the bad mother, bad daughter, bad friend. For just being bad—or so I thought. I had to learn to love my woman self, my black self, my poor self, my self that makes mistakes and always will.

Remember: you cannot be defined by a boyfriend, a job, your mother or father, rap music, television programs, newspapers or magazines. You were defined the day you were born. God has proclaimed you created in His image, capable of all things, deserving of the greatest blessings!

All you have to do is love your self enough to claim your glory.

7

The Real Mirror

◆

I am convinced that one of the greatest lessons I have to learn while here on this earth is the lesson evolving around choosing and loving a mate. I am in my fourth marriage, and while I know I have learned what seems like several lifetimes' worth of lessons about love, I know that I still don't understand it.

Yet one of the things I've learned is that love is not to be understood. At least on some level, I believe it is like God: incomprehensible. When my friend Donna asked me to write a verse to read at her wedding, I meditated, and the first words that came to me were: "Love is a three letter word, *G-o-d.*"

Love, I believe, is the manifestation of God. It is our lifeline to that other world, a glimpse of perfection, when we are one with God.

When we look at the person we date or marry, we should see the face of God. When we stand beside that person, our hearts should sing in rejoicing: "I am so blessed!" If we see something different, if what we feel is sadness and fear, then we are not existing in love.

So many times, I did not see God in the face of my lover or husband. Instead of looking more closely, I spent hours rationalizing why I should stay with the man: "He is nice. He needs me. He can't help himself." I did not know that neither love nor God needs rationalization.

We think love demands so much of us. If we really understood it, we would find it demands nothing.

* * *

When we look at the person we are dating, we are looking in a mirror. Hopefully, you like what you see. Your mate is a mirror of your soul. I used to think this meant that I and the man I was dating had to be exactly alike; that the person I would marry would be someone with the same political views, the same style of dressing, someone who liked to eat what I liked. If I saw the slight difference between me and my man, I changed *me*!

I was wrong. We are all different—and once we accept that, we will appreciate and even enjoy some of those differences. Of course, we must define what we can and cannot live with, but we don't have to like the same music and food. These are surface, earthly details. It is more important to me that my mate believe in God, understand the importance of family, be kind and respectful to other human beings.

I really didn't understand this—not fully—until I met my current husband. We are very different. He is much more conservative about life in general. I indulge; he lays back. I leap and he is cautious. I buy diet foods; he eats fats and sugar.

But we both love and enjoy the beauty of black theater and art as well as the beauty of nature. We like quiet evenings at home, family traditions, entertaining friends and relatives. He's funny, protective, interesting, is kind and loves family—and he believes in God.

When I met him, I needed to learn tolerance, particularly of people who did not believe in everything I believed in. I needed to learn that two people could be different yet have much in common. I knew this on one level, but I had never tested this lesson or used it in my own life. This is when a person you date becomes a mirror, too. When I looked at the man who is now my husband, I saw what I needed to learn, what he could teach me with his presence. It wasn't so clear, at first. But the longer we were together, the more I learned about life and myself.

The person you date is a mirror because that person will bring into your life the spiritual lessons you need to learn. They don't do it alone. You play a major part by choosing them. Also, it will be the two of you together, the combination of you and this other person, that make certain spiritual lessons possible.

Some of these lessons will be painful, others will bring you great joy. There may be a lesson teaching you that what you need to do is move on and leave this person. Or, you may learn that you need to be less selfish and to listen more.

One of my main problems has been that I am in love with love. I am in love with that feeling you get when you begin to care intensely for someone you're dating and you feel they love you. There is a period of magnified exhilaration and joy that can sometimes be unnerving or unsettling, almost unearthly. I love that feeling!

But rather than acknowledge my love for love, I denied it. Loving love is foolish, I thought—and I did not want to be foolish. But who was I fooling? Each time I felt this exhilaration I believed I was in love.

Now what I believe is that I was indeed feeling love, but that doesn't mean it was the kind of love that meant I should keep the person around. It didn't mean I should continue to date him or consider marriage.

Each time I began to date a man who was nice to me in the smallest way—who took me to dinner, enjoyed my company, or was kind—I got in the mood for love. In other words, I was in a state of being where I was open to love. When we are in the mood for love, I believe it is as if we have the palms of our hands turned upward, toward the sky and God. We are like antennas, and when we are ready to receive love, when we are in the right frame of mind and spirit, with our hearts open and extended—we can feel love. We can feel God.

But true love, the kind that sustains a relationship, is more than feeling love. We may have tapped into God because we are ready. Therefore, we could have felt love even though we were with someone who we should not spend our entire life with.

Let me explain this another way. The most powerful feeling of love I have ever felt was not even between me and someone I was dating. It happened while I was interviewing a woman—and I will always believe that somehow I was able to tap into the love that she and her husband felt for each other.

I was writing about this woman, who at almost forty years of age, was running in her fifth Boston marathon. I asked about what encouraged her, and I'll never forget that she said, "My husband, who believes I can do anything, is my encouragement."

As she began to describe the love they shared, I felt an overwhelming sense of contentment spread over me. It was a warm feeling of peace greater and more intense than anything I had ever felt. I was temporarily transformed and suspended in time. I did not believe I heard her with my ears, but inside my head and throughout my body. I was in their world, engulfed by the radiance of their love for each other. An intense heat came from inside of me, and I looked down at my palms because they felt so warm I thought they were glowing.

As all of this was happening, an inner voice said to me clearly: "You are feeling the love between this woman and her husband. This is what God's love feels like."

I did not mention the incident to anyone. If I had felt this while I was with a man, I would have thought I was in love. But because of the circumstances, I simply thought, "This is love." It did not mean I should spend the rest of my life with this woman.

The love I felt did not die when my interview with that woman ended. Love does not die. It exists always in many different ways.

I have often heard women say "But I love him" as they try to understand how they could still love someone who mistreats them. They say this particularly when trying to muster up the courage, faith, and strength to leave or walk out of an affair or marriage.

"That's fine," I advised a friend recently. "You can still love him. But leave him. Sometimes we love people who we have to leave."

My daughter reminds me that when she was a teenager I was fond of saying, "Love is not enough. I have interviewed too many men who when I ask, 'Why did you kill her?' have answered, 'Because I loved her.' "

What I advised my daughter was to pay attention to how someone treated her and not to be fooled by what they said—or even by her own love for them.

Ask yourself, "Does he treat me like he loves me?" "Does he treat me like he cares and respects me?"

For much of my life, I thought my father did not love me because he never said, "I love you." I carried the pain of my misconception into relationship after relationship, requiring that the men I dated—and married—say, "I love you." Most often, they obliged me. I made men who only wanted to have sex with me say it. I made men who did not even know what love was say it. And I, a woman desperate for the love of a man, said it frequently and far too easily.

So men came into my life who taught me how useless those three words can be with nothing to back them up. They mouthed the words I wanted, then they raped me, cheated on me, lied to me, and abused me in many, many ways.

My friend Fran's father, Bernard Sauve, is one of the wisest men I know. At seventy-six, he has been married to Fran's mother, Margaret, for forty-nine years. Once he shared with me a letter he wrote in 1984 to a friend—and I would like to share part of it here because it says all you really need to know about love.

> Shortly before you began your current exile into the northlands to continue nursing studies, you mentioned your disappointment in the fact that the fellow to whom you are engaged has a tough time indeed in getting out the words "I love you."
>
> Perhaps your disappointment lies in the fact that you may be so desperately listening for words that you are ignoring the fact. The word *love* is perhaps the most misused and abused in the English language. As commonly used today it connotes lust or personal gratification—something far removed from the beautiful meaning it is intended to convey.
>
> This is perhaps why a whole generation of young people—men mostly—have grown wary of using the term. Yet love is a very meaningful fact of life. The fact is that there is many a way of expressing love

without the trite use of words. Some songwriters seem to have grasped this point: "Touch my hair as you pass my chair . . . Little things mean a lot."

At St. James Church in Bay City a few weeks ago Father Wolfgang Streichard said in effect that . . . many a young couple thinks it has total love at the beginning of marriage, while in reality it has but the seed which can grow into a deeper and deeper love with the passage of time.

I remember as a child observing a habit of my father's. When we were at the dinner table—and there were a lot of us—my father would reach over into the meat dish and pull out a particularly savory bit, which he would place on my mother's plate. He did this consistently. It was his way of saying "I love you"—something his French-Canadian nature would never permit him to put into words.

I can see love all about me in my own life—and without being expressed in words. When I am tired in the evenings and lie back in my chair newly provided by my daughters, it is not long before my wife comes over and puts a warming blanket over me. It's her way of saying "I love you." When my oldest daughter comes home and nearly kills herself painting my kitchen, it's a repeat "I love you." When my No. 2 daughter comes home for a brief vacation and spends her few days working like a dog to clean up the debris around the house, she's saying "I love you." When my older brother Norm goes to the hospital to see his sick wife at six in the morning, at noon, and at intervals before nightfall—he's saying

"I love you." And when his wife tells him to go out and get a good meal, she's replying "I love you, too."

What I guess I'm trying to say, Mary, is don't worry so much about words. Let the facts of love speak for themselves.

I had to learn the lessons in this letter—and men came into my life who set about creating circumstances, often damaging ones, that taught me. I say "came into my life," but actually I chose them, just as you will choose the people you will share your life with.

I am still in love with love. Yet somehow acknowledging that truth about myself allows me to understand that I need to be especially cautious so that I will not be swept away by the exhilarating feeling alone. I still have to use my spiritual wisdom in choosing. I can't let the feeling rule me or choose for me. But if I let my heart, my head, and my eyes decide and have supreme faith, then choosing will be effortless.

Love should be fun. We should be learning about love each day of our lives, so that we know what is and isn't love. What love feels like. What love looks like.

Watch the people around you express love. Learn from praying, from knowing God. Don't be distracted by rap music, Hollywood, soap operas, or other earthly offerings that are merely entertainment, not spiritual sustenance.

Remember: love exists in our lives at all times, even if we feel especially alone because we do not have a significant other. Love is all around us and inside of us. Even when we think we have fallen out of love, love is there; we simply are not tuned into it.

Relax. Enjoy love. It is another path to teach us, another way for us to receive grace. In the end, we use our mighty power to choose, to decide who will be an instrument of love in our lives.

Use your spiritual rules, your understanding of God and of the kind of life each of us is entitled to by birth, to choose wisely.

8

Beyond
Romance

When I was consumed by my determination to find the right romantic partner, I didn't have time to think about the condition of the world or even the block on which I lived.

I was so busy scheming and trying to figure out how to get some guy over to my house, and then worrying about what to cook for him and what to wear, that I didn't have time to develop a social consciousness or a concern for anything outside my door. It is possible to do both: to search for a mate and have a sense of humanity. But when you are as consumed as I was, convinced that happiness is outside of yourself and that you've got to find it, you can't focus on anything else. I was on a mental treadmill, running but going nowhere, focusing on the same spot, yet unable to see what was in front of me.

What did I care about the trees being cut down, whether or not my neighbors had food to eat, or if troubled teens had someone to talk to. Don't get me wrong. I had my own sense of humanity. In my early twenties I had been an assistant scoutmaster when the church I attended needed someone so badly a friend begged me to help out. And I prayed for those less fortunate than me and felt great compassion for them. Yet, I seldom took action to help anyone. My attention stayed focused on myself and my own predicament.

But as my life began to change, so did my actions. During extended periods of peace—when my frantic search for a mate subsided—I reached out to others, and my world broadened. While I was living with my girlfriend Gaile, we worked in a political campaign to elect a black city council member.

During one particular period, while in my third marriage, I had a Halloween party for a local chapter of Easter Seals. I was working for the *Charlotte Observer* newspaper and learned that the chapter did not have a location for its annual Halloween party for children. I offered my house and gathered my friends together, assigning roles and responsibilities. There was something different going on in every room. One friend told fortunes, another was a fairy godmother. A magician performed, and to help them bob for apples I picked up and held children who were wearing heavy leg braces. I had informed everyone on my street that the kids would be trick-or-treating. They all cooperated, handing out candy and walking out their doors to the sidewalk to meet the children in wheelchairs.

I still smile when I remember that evening. I probably remember it more fondly than the children—because in many ways I got more from it than they did. They got candy, laughs, and hopefully, a memory or two. But I got a warm, long-lasting sense of peace and satisfaction I can still tune into at will. I also received a small, lovely potted plant from a young boy in a wheelchair, but years after the plant died, the joy of its giving remains in my soul.

*   *   *

Giving can heal the giver. I had a friend who had just broken up with a man she had dated and lived with for a number of years. Their separation was sudden and not her choice, so the pain, understandably, was quite unsettling. As we talked about her healing, she asked me if I had some books that might help as she healed. I loaned her a few and offered some homegrown wisdom. For a while, I remembered to pray for her daily, because I wanted to see her free of pain; she is a wonderful spirit, someone I respect and love. A short while later, she asked if she could use me as a reference because she was going to become a volunteer at a shelter for women who had been abused. When she told me this, I knew she was headed in the direction of healing.

Why? Because in a practical sense, at least for the period that she was giving, she would be too busy helping others to think about her own pain. She would find herself thinking about the women she was helping—even when she was at home, even during those night hours when she would otherwise cry because of her own pain. Her giving would not erase her suffering, but slowly the giving would become more important than the grief. I knew, too, she was going to find lessons in the lives of those women, lessons that would help her in her own life. She was on her way to a spiritual school disguised as a shelter for women.

Perhaps she went to the shelter to find something to soak up her thinking time, a diversion from her self-pity. But giving can teach us so much. Sometimes I think all of us are ready to give of ourselves at those times, such as the period my friend found herself in, when we need healing ourselves. It seems that these are the moments when we are likely to give unabashedly. When we need to be healed is when we are able to fling ourselves into the spiritual sea to rescue someone else, to give passionately and relentlessly. I believe, too, that it is then, when we are at our emotionally lowest point, that we're in a state of intense sensitivity to others, our receptors are open, our hands cupped upward toward God in prayer. We have been humbled by our own pain.

Some months after my friend had moved to another city because of a job transfer, I had an occasion to visit the women's shelter where she had volunteered. Everyone who found out that I knew her asked me about her. "She was our best tutor," one woman said. "She was my favorite," said another. "I hope she comes back," said a third.

I smiled, knowing that they had left their own indelible marks on my friend's heart, too. They gave her lessons that have helped her make better decisions in the future, and through the combination of her giving and their receiving (and giving, too) she was healed.

Over the years, as my life changed, I developed a sense of oneness, a real feeling that we are all connected, regardless of color, education, locale, or any of the other superficial distractions that might make us think we are not one. When I speak to large groups, I often begin my presentation by asking everyone to breathe deeply—together. Then I talk about how we breathe the same air; how the air I breathe has passed through many lungs and how the people present will breathe in air that has flowed through my veins. The very act of breathing reminds us that we are divinely connected. Before I reached this understanding, I would walk into a store and steal anything I wanted. If it could fit under my dress or coat, in my pocketbook or a bag, it was mine. If I visited your house, I stole anything I wanted. I have learned better. Now I am more likely just to enjoy the pretty things you have and pay attention to how you have arranged them; I can appreciate what all these things say about who you are. I believe everything has a vibration, and if I am still, I can feel it all and know to some degree what you are trying to convey with the items you have chosen to have around. I will never steal again.

What made me change? My sense of oneness evolved, and in a way it sneaked up on me. I changed so many fibers of my being that I became a new person. And in my newness, I understood that when I steal from someone, I steal from myself. Because we are truly one. This understanding was a by-product of change, a gift of grace.

* * *

I turned away from the world, from my outward search, and went inside to find the God within me. I spent time with myself. By myself. I found that the answers—to happiness, peace, joy—are within and not in any person or thing. So that even if I owned what you own, stole all that you have, whether it is a drug, a ring, or a jeweled box (some of the things I remember stealing), none of this would satisfy me or make me happy. I achieved this moment of grace only by working hard to turn my life around. By forgiving myself and others. So that now I respect all— each and every person—that God has created.

When I was an assistant scoutmaster, I was going through the motions of helping others, but I never really felt I was helping. I had volunteered because someone I owed a favor asked me to do it, and I didn't know how to say no. I certainly did not give with a cheerful heart. I never received that by-product of peace, which makes me wonder if I ever really helped any of those little boys in my troop.

There is something to be said about giving with a cheerful heart. Perhaps it is another state of being that opens up the channels through which good flows back to us.

One afternoon as I sat in my car talking with a friend, a homeless man walked up to my window. I rolled down the window a little, and he said something like, "Can you help me out today?" I was irritated by the intrusion on our conversation. I reached down to the console and picked up a dime, the only coin there, and gave it to the man without even looking at him. I was clearly showing him by my body language that I just wanted him to get lost.

To my surprise, the man refused the coin. He put up

his hand and waved it away, as if to say "no thank you." I kind of shrugged, went on with my conversation and thought little of the exchange.

The next afternoon I was sitting on a park bench at lunchtime waiting for someone I was to interview when I noticed out of the corner of my eye another homeless person, a young man who looked to be in his mid-twenties. My first thought was: "Don't walk over here." Then I decided to change my thought: "If he comes, I'm going to talk to him like he is just another person, not like he is homeless." I didn't want anything in my manner to make him think I considered him any different from the next human being.

The guy came over, of course. I smiled. He saw my braces and flashed a big smile with the worst-looking mouth I've ever seen. His teeth were yellow and brown, terribly stained, and he had some kind of thick wire all across them.

"These aren't braces," he said, laughing. "A man punched me. We were arguing. He broke my jaw. I had to get it wired."

"Sounds painful," I said.

"Not anymore," he said. "That's why I didn't go back to the hospital."

"You should get it checked," I said, wincing uncontrollably, not only from thoughts of the pain but also because he smelled pretty bad—and because I wanted him to close that horrible-looking mouth. But I composed myself, remembering my promise.

"Would you have any money to help me buy lunch?" He hesitated a second, then pointing to a vending truck, he added, "I'm going right over there to buy a hot dog."

He was probably used to people thinking he was begging money to buy liquor or drugs. I gave him a dollar.

Before he walked away, his personality changed. "I believe I could change my life for you," he said, flirting.

"Don't change for me. Change for yourself," I said, quickly slipping into one of my philosophy speeches.

"Oh, don't do that to me," he said, serious again.

I quickly understood. He just wanted to be a "regular" guy flirting with a woman. For a split second I considered how long it must have been since a woman on the street just let him be a "regular" guy and had not been offended at his come-ons.

I gave him the pleasure of a return flirt. "I bet you would change for me," I said.

He smiled, and as he walked over to the truck, I considered the fact that I had just flirted with a homeless man. He bought a sandwich. Then I watched him as an elderly man dressed in a dark blue work uniform greeted him. When the elderly man, who must have been on his lunch hour, sat on a bench to eat a sandwich, the young homeless man sat with him. I noticed, though, that he did not sit right next to the elderly man but sat at one end of the bench while the older man sat at the other. I was impressed because it seemed to me the homeless man did this out of respect. He knew that his clothes were dirty and he smelled. I was touched, too, by how comfortable the old man was with the homeless man. The two talked and laughed like old friends.

After a while, I saw the guy with the wired mouth point over in my direction, as if he was talking about me. The old man looked at me and smiled. Then out of the corner of my eye, I saw the guy with the wired mouth walk over to a bed of flowers, bend down, and pick some of the flowers. I looked up to see him standing in front of me with his hands behind his back.

"Promise not to laugh at me," he said.

"I would never laugh at you," I said.

He pulled the bouquet of flowers from behind his back and handed them to me. "Th-th-this isn't much," he said, stuttering for the first time. "Y-y-you're a nice lady."

"Thank you," I said, rising to leave, giving up on meeting the person I was to interview.

"It's not for the dollar," he said. "Anybody could give me a dollar."

I was pondering those words as I walked away.

He must have had second thoughts because he said to himself, though loud enough for me to hear, "She'll probably throw them away."

I turned back to face him. "I would never throw them away. If I didn't want them, I wouldn't have taken them."

He winked, and as I crossed the street, walking away, he yelled, "I'd give up liquor for you, girl! I'll change my ways!"

I put the small bouquet of flowers in a vase on my desk, where they lasted for quite a while. But what will remain with me still longer are the questions and the lessons I asked myself: did it matter that I gave with a cheerful heart when I gave to the second homeless man? Did the first homeless man, the one at the car window, refuse my money because he felt my contempt? Why on two consecutive days did a homeless man approach me? It seemed divined, as if there was definitely something to learn.

Since meeting the second homeless man, I have tried to always give with a cheerful heart. I had known, since I was a child it seems, of the Bible verse in II Corinthians that says "God loveth a cheerful giver." But not until I met the two homeless men had I pondered the verse and the difference a cheerful heart can make in the circle of giving.

I used to think you had to give money to be rewarded for your giving. I ignored the importance of giving your time. But since then I have discovered that sometimes your time is of greater value to those who need help than your money could ever be. I enjoy using my time to speak to young teenage girls struggling with their sense of self-worth, with men and women trying to overcome drug addictions, with people learning to read, and with anyone in prison who wants to change. Basically, I understand that these people are "me" at another time in my life. I show up, and my appearance alone inspires them to believe that survival is possible.

You reach a plateau of universal love through forgiveness and compassion, by replacing blame with responsibility. When you are tied up by your own anger, by self-hatred or blaming others for your own state of being, you can't see beyond your fingertips. Everything centers around you, your wants and needs.

*　　*　　*

I was at a leadership conference for college students when I heard Greg Anderson, founder of the Cancer Conquerors, speak. He is a great motivational speaker, author of *The 22 (Non-Negotiable) Laws of Wellness* and other books about healing. Greg himself was diagnosed with metastatic lung cancer in 1984 and told he had thirty days to live. He is convinced he helped heal himself by changing the way in which he thinks and, therefore, lives.

When I heard him speak, he read a verse by Elton Trueblood entitled "On Leadership." But I think it could just as well have been called "On Life," and we should all think of ourselves as leaders in service to God. Basically the poem states that if you want to lead you should give, if you want joy you should give joy to others, and helping others will help you to achieve your own goals.

Many of us who understand complicated mathematical equations cannot grasp this simple spiritual concept: in order to receive, we must give.

*　　*　　*

While I was dating the man who is now my husband, he thought of me as a pushover, a sucker for a sob story. I was determined to prove that though I was a romantic and maybe a soft touch, I wasn't a sucker. I wanted to show my husband-to-be that there was a universal law available to everyone that said: "If you give, you shall receive."

One morning I was standing outside a department store, waiting for it to open so I could buy tickets to a concert. There were about twenty of us waiting, and when the store opened, we rushed to the ticket counter to form a line. When the young white woman in front of me reached the counter, she found that with service charge and taxes she was about eleven dollars short. I overheard her talking to the agent. She was buying a dozen or so tickets.

For a while, she stood there, trying to figure out what to do before she relinquished her cherished position at the front of the line. I sympathized with her, wondering whether she would have to go home, get more money, and return another day. What if they sold out? How far away did she live?

I decided to loan her the eleven dollars. Already, I had asked myself: Can I afford to give her the money? Will I be able to handle it—financially and mentally—if she never repays me?

So I offered the money. Before I could explain it was a loan, she said, "I'll pay you back. Give me your address."

Later that evening, I told my boyfriend about the incident. He said something like, "And you think you're going to get your money back, huh?"

"Yeah," I said. "I'm sure of it."

Less than a week later I received a thank-you note from the young woman. Inside was my eleven dollars as well as a twenty-five-dollar gift certificate to a boutique that I had often admired but never had the money to shop in. I added what seemed a reasonable sum of money to the certificate and was able to purchase a dress I adored.

I would never know the young woman if I saw her again, and I don't think she would know me. What does it matter.

The afternoon I received her note, I ran to show my boyfriend. I was thinking that this was certainly proof that you will get as good as you give.

*   *   *

We have to be willing to give not only to our relatives or people we love (that's easy most of the time), but we must also give to strangers, too. We must give, regardless of race, sex, sexual orientation, or social status. In fact, often-times I think we learn more by giving to those who are totally unlike us.

Each time I give I can almost see the blessings pouring back on me. Shortly after separating from my second husband, I needed some pieces of furniture for my new apartment. I needed a coffee table but had very little money, so I knew the table would have to be given to me or cost practically nothing. Instead of worrying about it or all the other things my child and I needed, I volunteered my time, giving motivational talks to groups of people who needed to hear my life's story. The stories I heard from the members of my audiences inspired me to have faith. So I measured the space where my new coffee table would set and envisioned myself receiving it. Within a couple of weeks, my brother-in-law called to say the furniture store where he worked was throwing out some damaged furniture, including a glass and brass coffee table missing one screw. Of course, it had the exact dimensions I needed—and my brother-in-law went out and got a screw and fixed it for me!

Another time, I needed a sofa. I went to take my mother and a friend to a storage company. While there, we drove past a Dumpster, and next to it stood a small sofa bed that looked to be in good condition. My mother asked the manager about it and he said, "You can have it, if you cart it away."

When $2,000 of my daughter's college tuition was due and I didn't have the money, her former employer loaned us the money. I explained the dilemma one day, and the woman had the check delivered the next. She told me I could repay her whenever I was able.

Before I discovered this divine law of giving, I had to go to a social services department in Charlotte, North Carolina, to ask for food. Once, I almost had to beg for medical treatment because I made seventy-nine dollars over the cutoff to be eligible for free medical care. But all of this seemed to change as I gave.

We must give to live. We may think we can make it alone in this life, but we can't. We all need each other, and once we broaden our vision by changing our focus from one that is self-centered to one that is God-centered, we then can begin to understand this.

I liken the effect of giving to a snowball. As the snowball rolls, it touches the snowflakes in its path, which make the snowball grow. That touching keeps it alive. Only when it stops, or when there is no more snow to gather up, does the snowball die. And so it is with us. We are called upon to touch others. Try living without giving and what you will have is not really life. You will melt—slowly—only you may not know it until your soul nearly vanishes.

Properly centered, understanding my oneness with every living creation (including the birds, trees, and even the rocks), I can enjoy this world as I never could when I was shooting heroin. On cold nights, I pray for the people and animals that do not have shelter. On rainy days, I enjoy the rain, which I used to think would make my day gloomy. I pick up litter thrown by strangers and give money to people who come up short in the grocery line. Life is much more enjoyable! I am blessed!

* * *

On my first trip to the Martin Luther King Jr. Center for Social Change in Atlanta, Georgia, I bought a postcard I have kept near my desk for years. Its verse reminds me of what I am capable of doing and inspires me to want to try. It quotes Dr. King and—in part—says: "Everybody can be great. Because anybody can serve. You don't have to have a college degree to serve. You don't have to make your subject and your verb agree to serve. You only need a heart full of grace. A soul generated by love."

9

What About the Divine?

◆

"When I was shooting heroin, I was searching for God."

I heard myself speaking these words to an audience one afternoon and I had no idea where they had come from. I mean, I had not planned to say this, and I had never had this thought before, at least not consciously. It was not a line in the prepared speech I had worked on the evening before. But as soon as I had spoken the words, I knew they were true.

Sometimes we have too narrow a definition of the paths people can take to find God. True, I was looking in all the wrong places. But I wasn't shooting drugs just because I liked the way heroin made me feel. On one level, this is what I thought. Yet, I knew, too, that I was totally dissatisfied with what I referred to as "this horrible existence called life." I could not see any purpose for living, any reason to go on.

"This can't be all there is," I thought when I considered all of my days up until that moment.

Since that time, I have seen many people experiencing the same kind of pain I was living through: young men toting high-powered guns with rocks of crack in their pockets; scantily clad young women standing in icy weather, offering their bodies for the price of a fix. Even if they don't know it, they're all searching for God.

*   *   *

I am not a theologian, so I will not attempt to explain God. I can only talk about my relationship to Him. In fact, I was baffled about the sex of God, so after pondering the question, I decided that although I refer to God as "Him" I mean to encompass the masculine as well as the feminine. I do this because of the imprecision of language. There is no pronoun that would describe a Divine Spirit that I believe is neither female nor male but is both—and yet much more. We have a limited definition of sex, but I also believe we have a limited understanding of it.

*   *   *

When my daughter was about four or five, at the age when it seemed every other word out of her mouth was "Why?", she used to ask lots of questions about God. Many of them I could not answer; many I answered differently than anyone else she asked. To try to lessen my child's confusion, I explained to her: "You will have to find out who God is for yourself. That is part of what life is about. It is about finding God."

I still believe this. Each of us has to develop our own

personal relationship with God. I grew up attending a Baptist church, going to Sunday school sometimes, singing in the youth choir. Most often, my parents did not go with us children to church. Mom dressed us and sent us on our way. But she also taught us the importance of prayer. At one point in my life, I remember Mamma praying with us before we left for school each morning. She had us get on our knees to pray at night, too. And, of course, we never ate a bite of food without blessing it.

Later, in my early twenties, I went to church irregularly, and I almost stopped going altogether. God was not popular with me or my peers. In the 1960s, I think most of the young black people I knew were turned off by the pictures in many churches depicting Jesus as white. "If Jesus is white, what color is God, his father?" I wondered.

I remember once telling my grandfather I was going to join his Baptist church. Over the years, I used to enjoy services there, before I had moved away and was unable to attend the church. When I returned to Washington, I returned to the church with my grandfather. But now that I was older, I could not take my eyes off the huge mural behind the altar depicting Jesus as a white man. I did not join the church, and yet I could not find the words to explain to my grandfather why.

Also, from what I saw and heard in the fire-and-brimstone sermons there, I could not imagine God being approachable or my friend. The God I heard about—a fearsome, distant spirit—could not be a part of a young black girl such as myself.

By the time I was in my midtwenties, I embarked on a deliberate search to understand God. I was driven after a moment of peace, a period of time when I was not frantically searching for a man. I was also encouraged by a good roommate-sister-friend who was in the midst of her own quest to find God. We read books on religion, spiritualism, philosophy, love, and even on positive thinking. It was during this time that I began to believe—and see—that I was godly, too, that there existed in me the power to do things that could not be explained by the conventional religious doctrine I had heard all my life.

I prayed, fasted, and meditated regularly, and it was in my stillness that the inexplicable happened. I had visions that came true, I wrote down pages and pages of thoughts and verses, which seemed to come from my mind, only to find them later, exactly as I had written them, in books I had never read. My roommate, Gaile, and I dreamed dreams that came true and seemed to be able to know each other's thoughts.

To me, these were signs of the presence of God. This was what could happen with devotion and when I was still enough to tune out the world and tune in God. This is what could happen when peace resides in a house, a family, a relationship. Heaven was no longer a place where I would go if I was good; it was a state of being, and I had felt a glimpse of it during these moments of grace.

So my relationship with God evolved. I began to talk to Him. The Spirit that I feared and felt no part of as a youth had been replaced in my heart by a Spirit who is my partner and friend. One that was approachable and always present. I developed a personal relationship with God. Sometimes I fussed at Him. Sometimes I laughed at Him. It was no longer difficult to pray because I was praying to a friend. I was new. Forgiven.

*　　*　　*

Over the years, I have visited many churches of various denominations. In each church, whether it was Catholic, Baptist, Unitarian, or Spiritual, I found a universal truth there that spoke to me. I joined a Baptist church with an emphasis on Afro-centric services. Now that I've married a man who is Catholic, I have studied Catholicism and attended Catholic churches. I also enjoy attending a church that is a member of a group called the National Spiritualist Association of Churches. I don't worry about what denomination I am anymore. I seldom feel like a stranger in any church.

*　　*　　*

As my relationship with God has developed, I have learned to relax more, to laugh more often. I spent much of my life struggling. Fighting for my father's love. Fighting to keep a husband. Fighting for jobs I believed I was being denied because of racism. Whenever I was focused on the battle at hand, there was no peace. Standing there dressed in my mental and spiritual armor, I was standing in the way of God's light, blocking my own good.

So I began to fight in a different way, by giving up every problem to God. By saying things like, "Okay, God, I don't even understand what is going on here, so how could

I possibly straighten it out. You do what you do and I'll pray and not worry," Or, "God, obviously these people don't want me here because I am black, but since racism is not from you, I am going to treat it as nonexistent. You handle it, and I will use the power you have given me to change what I can."

This doesn't mean you don't act, or that you let people tread all over you. By recognizing your God-given powers, you trust that God will clue you in on whether or not the job is worth wanting, or whether or not you should use your power to walk away.

It was no longer enough to blame racism or any factor outside of me for the conditions in my life. Instead, I acknowledged those challenges while knowing in my heart that God is greater than all of them. God and I are eternal partners. If I do my best, a door opens. I have learned to fight in a quiet, grace-filled way. And now, mountains move.

Sometimes this has meant walking away. Yet I knew I was not running, or retreating. Sometimes staying to fight only increases the friction. By being still, God will speak to you. But you must listen.

* * *

Once I was less tolerant of others when they did not believe as I do. Denying them respect, friendship, a decent word—whatever—was another way of fighting. Now I have two friends who say they do not believe in God. The old, I-know-what's-right me would have been outraged. But my friends' beliefs have never made me love them less. They are married and have children and all of them—the husband and wife and their children—seem to live by God's laws. They are kind, compassionate, honest, and trustworthy people who work to serve others. I tease them, saying, "You all believe in God and you don't even know it."

I imagine when they make their transition from the earth and unite with God that even the Spirit will chuckle and say, "You never called me by name—but you called me."

*   *   *

Some people can make great changes without believing in God. I am not one of them. I needed to know God. He made sense out of my incomprehensible world.

I remember as a teenager thinking I did not want a God like the one my grandmother worshipped. She was a God-fearing woman, but I always felt she sat and waited for God to change things for her. Now, I know my perceptions may have been a little warped because my grandmother scaled incredible challenges, including a third grade education, to raise my mother and send her to college. Still, as a child, it did seem to me that Grannie expected God to do anything she wanted while she just sat on her little red stool and looked out the window.

As a teen, I wanted to scream at her, "Do it yourself!" Though I did not know yet that we have God-power inside us, I had a sense that God would help us if we helped ourselves.

I have assured women in prison that God is keeping safe their talents until they are ready to use them. The talent that saved me was writing. My partner held it for me until I was ready to respect it and use it. Surely, I would have lost it or squandered it if it had been left in my care while I was lost.

It meant everything to me to know a divine and pure love exists, that I am never alone. That it does not matter how the world sees me because I am perfect. There exists as a part of my being an element of perfection that I can tune into with faith, devotion, and prayer.

God frees us from any limitation. We are no longer a minority, poor, too fat, or too tall. We are more than what we see or what others see when they look at us.

* * *

I have learned a lot about God from death.

When my mother was sick, many people prayed for her to be well, meaning free of cancer, so she could live and remain with us. Of course, we did not want to let go.

But my daughter, wise beyond her years, asked, "What should we pray for?"

I had asked myself the same question and was not sure I had an answer, so we shared our confusion about how to pray. We agreed that people who wanted her cured seemed steadfast in their belief that life here on earth was what was best for her. And also, most seemed confident that only a cure would mean their prayers had been answered.

But Andrea and I decided to pray that God's will be done and that we somehow find the grace to accept it. We prayed for Mom's peace. I asked my daughter: "If God is so good, why would I not want my mamma to be with God?

Why should I, in my selfishness, seek to deny her that peace?"

I understood that those who prayed that Mother live were asking this out of love. I did not want her to suffer either. I was pleased when she said she did not feel pain but that she was "tired." I had heard that word uttered by friends who had died of AIDS. They would say, "I am so tired," or something like that, shortly before they closed their eyes for the last time. It is tiring when you are trying to fight to stay alive.

We all struggle too much sometimes. And in so doing, we get in the way of God. I have accepted that the pain we feel in grieving is an unavoidable part of being human. And this grief is inevitable until we reach the understanding that death is not terrible but is a wonderful reward for having endured this life, that death is a natural part of the cycle.

When it was my mother's time to leave, I sat beside her bed and whispered, "Go and be with God."

I am trying to learn to struggle less, to be more accepting of God's will. To understand that babies will be born into my family and people I love will die. To accept the joy and the pain with equal thanksgiving and understanding. I am trying to let go and let God enter every molecule of my being now, before I am too tired.

10

When You Get to the End of the Rope Tie a Knot and Hang On

◆

By the time I reached my senior year of high school, I had already survived syphilis, a car accident, hitchhiking with strangers, hooking school, and a whipping from my father. The syphilis, given to me by my first love, landed me in the intensive care ward of a hospital. During the car accident, late one night on rain-slicked "snake road," my life flashed before my eyes, but I walked away with only a sore neck and shoulders.

When my senior year came, I was counting my blessings, feeling pretty lucky to have made it that far. Of course, I hadn't focused on school enough to have a prepared quote for the yearbook. When the day came to decide what quote I wanted printed under my picture, I considered some of the sayings used by other seniors. One particular quote grabbed me, so I copied it. Under my photo in the DuVal Senior High School Class of 1967 Yearbook, you will find: "When you reach the end of your rope, tie a knot and hang on!"

*   *   *

I had not worked out the finer details of life, such as whether or not I would ever go to college, what I wanted to be, or where I wanted to live. I had no direction or goal. The only thing I had going for me was a zest for life that told me regardless of what lay ahead, I had to keep on stepping. I would not give up.

Perseverance appealed to me. Somehow I knew it would be perseverance that would separate those who succeeded from those who failed. Sure, there were other factors that would make some of us reach our goals before others. But the sheer ability to hang in there, it seemed to me, would just wear down every kind of resistance or challenge you would face.

*   *   *

I come from a long line of women who persevered. I remember going with my grandmother to make what would be her last visit to see her sister, my Aunt Letha. Grannie, who was sixty-nine, walked haltingly, taking just a few steps then stopping to get her breath, her nearly useless arms dangling at her side. She had suffered several strokes, and her thoughts and words came at an unsteady pace, sometimes fast, sometimes painfully slow. At seventy-three, Aunt Letha was blind, her darkness brought on by her diabetes.

My grandmother made her way up a flight of about six steps and into the living room where Aunt Letha waited, seated on the sofa. Aunt Letha turned to face Grannie as she sat next to her.

Generations of younger folks, the two women's children and grandchildren, stood around, ready to break into tears any second. We recognized the poignancy of the moment, the fact that we would never see this again.

Aunt Letha was the first to speak. "Looking" at her sister and with a smirk on her face, she said, "You just as ugly as ever."

We were so shocked, some of us gasped.

"Don't make me jump over there and whip you," Grannie retorted.

"I'll beat the ugly off you, girl, talking to your elder like that," said Aunt Letha.

"And you think I'm going to just sit here and let you beat me. *Humph.* You're so craazzzy," Grannie said, purposely exaggerating the word *crazy*, as she had always done in the days before her stroke.

By this time, we had recovered enough to understand what was happening. These two feisty old women who were known for their sharp humor were not about to give in to sorrow and pain.

I think of that meeting every time I consider for one second the possibility of giving up on anything. I think of a woman who could not see and another who could barely move or breathe. I think of how they used what they could—laughter—to carry on. To persevere to the end.

* * *

For years I kept a folder called "Inspiration," where I filed away articles and sayings that encouraged me. Then on a bad day, when I needed a boost, I'd dig them out and read them again. I read an article recently that I would have filed in that folder if I still kept it. It was an article called "A Study in Perseverance," and it told the story of an accomplished twenty-nine-year-old man who was just learning to read.

As a child, Ian Charles had been tagged "learning disabled." He grew up damaged by the taunts of classmates and by well-meaning teachers who did not know how to teach him. But despite his wounded self-esteem, Ian harbored dreams of the kind of adult life he wanted, which included a family, a nice home, and a business. He was determined to have that life. So armored with endless faith, he set about creating it.

For years, he kept secret the fact that he could not read. Then finally, a cousin found out and gave Ian the number for the Literacy Council of Northern Virginia, where they would teach him to read. Ian called immediately.

By the time I met him, he had turned thirty and had been tutored in reading for nearly five years. He is a tall, lanky guy with a perpetual smile and a boyish face that makes him look young enough to be mistaken for a recent high school grad. Ian also has that almost contagious zest for life I find in people who beat the odds. He is happy, up-beat, and unruffled by any question or comment. He showed up with his four-year-old daughter, Tynika, and he handed me one of his business cards: "Charles Limousine Service, Ian G. Charles, President."

I had already read in the article about how one morning at home, in the wee hours of daylight, Ian was poring over his reading workbook when he came across words he could not figure out. Since his wife was asleep and it was too early to call anyone else, Ian dialed 411 and spelled the words to the operator, who pronounced them for him.

It was a metaphor for his life: whenever Ian wanted something, he found the person who could help him get it. His faith told him that even when it looked as if no one was present, there was always somebody; his job was to find them.

"Although I did not know my grandfather well—he lived in Tobago—he taught my mother, aunts, and uncles that if you believe in something, go for it. God will provide a way. That got passed on to me.

"Just watching my mom, I developed perseverance," said Ian. "She worked two jobs, did whatever she had to do. One time when I didn't have a car and was trying to get a job that was far, far away, she said, 'Get the job and God will provide.' Sometimes I used to shake my head and say, 'What is this woman talking about?' But I always did what she said."

He applied for the job and got it. Then, just as his

mother had predicted, God provided. Though he didn't think anyone would live as far away from the job as he did, he found out that a co-worker was his neighbor. Ian got a ride every day from his front door to the job.

"People say life is hard. But hard is the norm to me," he said. "Each day is a challenge. Life is just ups and downs. It is an ongoing struggle. But to me, I had one choice—and it was to succeed."

By acknowledging that life can be difficult, he has freed himself of the fear that so many people allow to paralyze them. The fear of bad times, of not being able to handle a problem; the worry over something you cannot change. Ian just accepts that life can be hard—and then he moves on.

Not being able to read, he had to devise creative ways to accomplish many tasks. His mother filled out his job applications. He worked mostly cleaning and construction jobs, where reading was not an issue. He got his driver's license by taking the test orally. He learned to memorize information, to observe carefully, and to copy what others did.

To become articulate, he listened to talk radio shows—and more recently, motivational speakers. When he was twenty and working two jobs, he decided what he wanted was a $25,000 white BMW. He was on one of his jobs, cleaning a bank after business hours, when he listened in on a training class for new employees. The teacher talked about credit, and Ian remembers hearing the message that the only way you can get money from a bank is if you prove you don't need it. He put away $200 every two weeks for the next year and a half to build up his bank account and prove to his credit union he was credit-worthy.

On his twenty-second birthday, Ian got a loan and bought his BMW!

When he decided to start his own limousine service, he bartered for information. When a businessman needed some furniture moved, Ian agreed to move it in exchange for advice on writing contracts. Again, he found that the bank would not give him a loan to buy a limo. Then he saw a television interview with Robert Townsend, in which the filmmaker said he financed his first movie with money from his credit cards. Ian did the same, scraping together the money for the limo from fifteen credit cards.

Now, even more confident of his future, Ian has joined a local Rotary Club made up of mostly male, white, middle-aged businessmen. Ian is young and black. In the company of men who own banks and multimillion-dollar international enterprises, his business with its one limo seems mighty small. But at his induction service, Ian told club members, "When I came here, I was thinking—I'm just like y'all."

He sees little difference between himself and the other members—only time, the time it will take him to have the successes they have had. He wants to become a motivational speaker and to enroll in a nearby community college one day. But he's got some major hurdles first. Adults learn reading more slowly than children. Ian was reading on just the third grade level when I met him.

Yet who can measure the power of perseverance?

Through his refusal to give up, Ian has already accomplished more than most of his classmates and teachers could have imagined for him.

"Over the years I learned you've got to love yourself," he said. "I was never the best at everything. I felt less than everyone, I fell short in everything. I could have believed I was nothing. But I wanted to be something. I wanted to be the best and have the best. Anything less was unacceptable.

"You have to believe you can succeed. Otherwise, you won't take credit for your accomplishments. You will think it's just luck."

Before he left me, Ian could not resist showing off his four-year-old daughter, Tynika, whom he has taught to read and write. He called out several sentences and she wrote each carefully and correctly. Then Ian paused to think. "I can't think of the other sentences," he sighed.

A moment later, Tynika's face lit up as she remembered one of the sentences Ian had taught her. She whispered: "God is good."

*　　*　　*

I went to a West Virginia college to speak once and met a young woman whose courage and perseverance impressed me so much that I developed a friendship with her, and she has become like an adopted daughter.

At twenty-one, Bonnie Honora Hammons is a junior, majoring in communications. She sat beside me at the reception dinner for the black student group, which she headed and which had brought me to the campus. But it was her question to me at the end of a press conference that captured my heart.

"What would you say to a young person who is having a difficult time?" Her voice faltered. She stuttered. The confident young woman with whom I had spent the evening had vanished.

"I mean, what can we say to encourage kids who may have to deal with drugs and violence in their neighborhoods." Her voice cracked again. "Maybe they have made some bad choices in the past . . ." Now she was struggling to hold back tears.

I rescued her with an answer. I don't remember what I said. I was transfixed by the image of her crumbling before my eyes. I wanted to know what could tear at her so. With my eyes, I begged her to tell me.

She waited until the reporters had left. Alone, I hugged her and she sobbed. Her brother was in trouble, she explained. Then she laid out the details of her life, which included growing up in a Texas housing project without a father and with a loving mother who was fragile and struggling with her own problems. Though Bonnie had made it out, earning a full scholarship to an expensive girls college, she worried about her two brothers and her mother.

That meeting between us was over a year ago, and in the months that have passed, I have come to greatly respect and admire Bonnie. At times she has been penniless, and yet she has never given up her determination to get a college education. When she couldn't afford books, she visited friends in their dorm rooms at night and studied from their books. At one point, she was working two jobs while attending college, and she still made the dean's list.

"My perseverance comes from watching my mother and grandmother, seeing my grandma scrub floors and my mother get off one job and go to another," Bonnie told me.

Yet indirectly, she learned another lesson from her mother's and grandmother's lives. "They were so sacrificing. They focused on the children. I always wanted to focus on myself, too, on what I can do for me. But people looked down on that attitude, especially in the South.

"I didn't care. I spent time with myself, by myself. When you do that, you get to know who you are."

One thing Bonnie became sure of was that she had come from people who were survivors. As a black woman, she drew on the history of her people to give her strength and perseverance.

"I have always felt that my ancestors, who were slaves, are with me. I talk to them. I look at how they survived the Middle Passage. My strength comes from all of that—and from God, who I talk to a lot—out loud.

"I never accept no for an answer. Anything is possible. I will not compromise my dreams for anybody. That gives me courage to walk into the president's office and say, 'I did this and this, so what can you do for me?'" And that is just what she asked her college president when she returned to school and was told she could not attend her classes until she paid a $2,000 balance. She told the president about her dean's list grades, her community and school activities, and her otherwise illustrious school record.

"I feel I deserve a good education, though I don't expect anyone to give me anything," said Bonnie.

What the college president did was postpone payment of the debt and allow Bonnie to get paid in cash for her work-study job instead of having the money go directly to the school, as usual.

Like most people who persevere, Bonnie believes she is entitled to blessings by the mere fact that she was created. Hard work never scared her. The day she turned fifteen, she went to work at Taco Bell, working twenty hours a week while attending high school, and participating in activities such as track and cheerleading. At sixteen, she became one of the youngest employees at her local Wal-Mart. Still, she graduated from high school in the top 2 percent of her class.

"I only had two dresses, one pair of jeans, and one pair of shoes," Bonnie recalled. "Even though I worked, I always had to help pay bills and help buy my brothers' school clothes and supplies."

Her wardrobe may have been lacking, but her self-esteem was not. Bonnie has always had a great sense of self-worth, though sometimes it was harder to hold on to it than at other times. As a kid, she was transferred to a predominantly white middle school outside of her neighborhood, a school for "the smart kids." Students laughed at the things she did not know. She remembers specifically sending the kids into hysterics when she asked a teacher, "What is a foyer?"

"We didn't have one at our house, so I never heard of a foyer," she said. Another teacher called her a "ghetto rat" and said she would never amount to anything. Then one day when she was in the bathroom at school she even overheard a black teacher telling another that Bonnie should not be allowed to join a social club. "She doesn't have a father, money, or any home training," the woman said.

Still, Bonnie persevered.

"I would always find a way to get my voice heard—if I had to stand in the middle of class and yell.

"I remember when I was about five and we lived in a shack, the raggediest house on the street. People laughed at me and said sarcastically, 'Are you all rich?' I would always say, 'Yes. We're very rich. We laugh, we sing, we have fun in my house.'

"As little as I was, I knew to equate richness with family and happiness," she said.

While other children in her neighborhood were lured into criminal activity by the promise of fast money, Bonnie said her dreams kept her straight. "I wanted to see more of the world. I didn't want anything to keep me right there."

Now she is attending college on an oratory scholarship that pays her $23,000 tuition a year. Still, she said, "I always have to wonder how I will buy things as basic as pencils, pens, and paper. It's always a struggle."

But Bonnie has no thoughts of giving up. She has persevered beyond poverty, tough streets, hatred, and racism.

She has the necessary humor to survive, the iron will to succeed, the faith to believe she can, the love for herself to claim her blessings.

*　　*　　*

My life is a lesson in perseverance. Over the years following school, I traveled a tumultuous path. I was a journeywoman with no map and no sense of direction. I survived heroin, rape, failed marriages, beatings, and emotional abuse. I remember a friend who I admired and who had known me for years once saying, "Patrice, what I always admired about you was that you never gave up."

I was stunned. Even though I had started out at the beginning of the race, at high school graduation, with the philosophy of holding on, I had long forgotten those words. I was so entangled in a web of self-hatred that I felt as if I was choking. I hardly remembered the me that graduated from high school.

And though my friend didn't know it, a few times I did think about giving up. It was a fleeting thought. I always found a reason to go on. At first, it was for my daughter. Then later, when I knew it wasn't fair to put such a burden on a child—and when I knew we have to live for ourselves—I kept going for me. I survived because I wanted to. If I could just tie a knot and hold on, I told myself, a better day would come. Things would change.

When I considered suicide, my next thought was always: But what if things change tomorrow and I'm not here to see it?

During my period of horrific self-hatred, I had one

huge desire, one goal that kept me alive: I wanted to be somebody. Not a writer, a reporter, or an author. Other people had goals like that; I just wanted to think I was a person equal to everyone else. I wanted to believe I mattered to this earth. I wanted to believe I had worth.

This is what young men who deal drugs want. It is what young women who have babies when they are still babies want. It is what alcoholics, drug addicts, and people we consider sexually promiscuous want. They do not have time for other goals. What they want is love. The core of our being begs for it, whether we acknowledge it or not.

I was determined to be somebody. And the only way to do that was to persevere. Yes, for years I searched in the wrong places, but I was persistent in my search.

It was only when I began to read about a God who existed everywhere, including inside of me, that I began to feel worthy. Only after I meditated, prayed, had faith, and acted on that faith.

All the time, I had been searching for God. Yet I never would have known this if I had given up. I went far away from myself, as far out of my head as heroin would take me, only to return and discover I was somebody from the moment God breathed life into my spirit!

I was on a radio program when a woman caller alluded to her dreams and said to me, "But it's too late for me. I congratulate you for following your dreams."

"It's not too late. You are still breathing," I said.

*   *   *

We are capable of achieving great things. God made it so. We were born knowing this, but most of us forget at some point during our time on earth as we cope with drug addictions, death, cheating spouses, endless bills and budgets, and countless other distractions that can sway us from this truth.

You must be tireless, dogged, determined, and persistent in your search for a divine way of living. You must have an insatiable desire to live, so that even when your will wanes, when difficult times make you weak with pain, the part of you that wants to go on finds a reason to do so. Maybe it is watching an elderly woman, hunched over so far she can only look at her feet, make her way across a sun-lit street. Maybe it is seeing your child walk in from school, throw down his books in his home, and look at you as if he has arrived in the safest, most love-filled place on earth.

Life can be difficult. But the strength that boosts our will to persevere is with us every moment. You just have to open your eyes and your heart. You must not be blinded by worry over tomorrow, or over someone you cannot change, or over what may never be.

Seize this day, this moment. And if you choose to do the right thing now, if you just make a decision to try, then change begins. When the next moment comes, all you have to do is repeat that decision, maintain the course, and perseverance will take root and grow.

Faith is our gift from God. Perseverance is what we give back. We use our faith over and over, again and again, and it becomes what is known on this earth as perseverance. It's so simple: when you reach the end of the rope, just tie a knot and hang on. God will lift you up.

Afterword

Several months after I had finished writing *Moments of Grace*, I reread the original manuscript because I felt I needed the insight of some of those passages that day. As I read my words I had a revelation: I did not feel like the writer. Instead I felt as though I was reading those words for the first time. As I continued to read, I asked myself "How could I have been so sure of this on the day I wrote it—and yet feel so uncertain today? Where is that self-assured woman?" That is the way life is. You can feel strong one day, and on the very next, a sister, a coworker, or a complete stranger can piss you off or put you down and make you forget everything you've learned.

Each day brings with it tests and lessons. Some are new, but many are simply old lessons we've forgotten and need to be reminded of. That's why I can return to lessons in *Moments of Grace* and my words can seem like the words of a stranger; as if I were learning something completely new. It can be unsettling; but isn't that the way life is? You think you've learned something—finally—and you can put that lesson behind you. Then months later, you trip over a challenge and are reminded that no lesson is final unless we take care of the knowledge we have gained. We have to add to it, refine it, keep it shined, review it, and renew it.

This experience served as a reminder to me—again—that I am not only the teacher. If I have taught you anything with my words, it is only because, at times, I have been a very good student.

We are always teaching.

We are always learning.

And we are always changing.